Contents

Chapter 1: Understanding the Basics — 7

Chapter 2: Getting Started with Trading — 9

Chapter 3: Types of Investments — 12

Chapter 4: Fundamental Analysis — 14

Chapter 5: Technical Analysis — 17

Chapter 6: Candlestick Chronicles: Unraveling Market Dynamics — 26

Chapter 7: Mastering Breakout Patterns: Unleashing Market Momentum — 49

Chapter 8: Mastering Technical Indicators — 77

Chapter 9: Risk Management in Stock Trading — 92

Chapter 10: Making Money with ETFs, Mutual Funds, and IPOs — 95

Chapter 11: 5 Free tools For intraday trading — 99

DISCLAIMER

This book, "The Beginner's Blueprint to Stock Market Trading," is intended to provide introductory information and guidance for individuals interested in understanding the basics of trading in the stock market. The content within this book is for educational purposes only and should not be considered as financial, investment, or trading advice.

The author is not a licensed financial advisor, and the information presented in this book is based on general knowledge and experience in the field. Stock market conditions and regulations may change, and it is important for readers to conduct their own research or consult with a qualified financial professional before making any investment decisions.

The author and publisher make no representations or warranties of any kind, expressed or implied, about the completeness, accuracy, reliability, suitability, or availability of the information contained in this book. Any reliance on the information provided is at the reader's own risk.

Trading in the stock market involves inherent risks, and past performance is not indicative of future results. The author and publisher disclaim any liability for any financial loss or damage that may arise directly or indirectly from the use of the information provided in this book.

Readers are encouraged to seek personalized advice from a qualified financial professional and to carefully consider their own financial situation and risk tolerance before engaging in any trading activities. By reading this book, the reader acknowledges and agrees to the terms of this disclaimer.

Remember to consult with a legal professional to ensure that the disclaimer meets all necessary legal requirements and is suitable for your specific situation.

Chapter 1: Understanding the Basics

Welcome to the exhilarating universe of stock market trading, where financial opportunities abound! If you're new to this world, fear not; in this chapter, we'll unravel the mysteries of the stock market, laying the groundwork for your exciting journey into the realm of trading.

The Stock Market Unveiled

What is the Stock Market?
Picture a dynamic marketplace, a bustling hub where buyers and sellers converge. Now, substitute tangible goods with something intangible yet powerful: shares of ownership in companies. Congratulations, you've just stepped into the mesmerizing world of the stock market. It's a thriving ecosystem where investors engage in the buying and selling of securities, shaping the economic landscape on a global scale.
Why Does it Matter?
Understanding the stock market isn't just about grasping market dynamics; it's about comprehending its profound impact on the global economy. By providing companies with the means to raise capital, the stock market fuels innovation, stimulates growth, and offers you, the investor, an opportunity to become a part of this economic tapestry.

Key Terms for Beginners

Before we plunge into the intricacies, let's acquaint ourselves with some foundational terms:
1. Stocks: These are the building blocks of the market, representing ownership in a company. Also known as shares or equities, they grant you a stake in a company's success.
2. Dividends: Enjoy a share of a company's profits by receiving dividends. Some companies distribute a portion of their earnings

to shareholders, adding a valuable dimension to your investment.
3. Brokers: Picture brokers as your guides through the market maze. They facilitate the buying and selling of stocks, acting as intermediaries between you and the stock exchanges.

Exchanges: Platforms where the action unfolds. Think of them as the marketplaces where stocks are traded, such as the New York Stock Exchange (NYSE) and the Nasdaq.

These terms are the stepping stones to your stock market journey. As we progress, they'll become second nature, but for now, consider them the ABCs of your financial education.

Your Financial Journey

Setting Sail: Your Financial Goals
Every voyage needs a destination. Similarly, your financial journey begins by setting clear goals. Are you saving for a dream vacation, a home, or retirement? Your goals will serve as the compass guiding your investment decisions.

Your Financial GPS: Goal-Setting Exercises
In the accompanying workbook (accessible via the link at the end of this chapter), you'll find practical exercises designed to help you articulate your financial aspirations. These exercises aren't just academic; they're your personal financial GPS, navigating you through the twists and turns of the stock market.

Navigating the Ocean of Knowledge

Before we hoist the sails in the next chapter, take a moment to absorb the excitement of this venture. The stock market is not just a financial space; it's a dynamic ocean of knowledge, opportunity, and discovery. As you embark on this educational journey, keep in mind that the stock market is a vast, ever-evolving landscape. Embrace the learning process, and soon you'll be navigating the markets with confidence and savvy.

Happy reading, and let the adventure continue!

Chapter 2: Getting Started with Trading

Congratulations on taking the first steps into the thrilling world of stock market trading! In this chapter, we'll navigate through the practical aspects of setting up your journey, from choosing the right brokerage platform to establishing your trading account.

Selecting a Brokerage Platform

Understanding Your Options:
In India, the financial landscape offers a variety of brokerage platforms, each with its unique features and advantages. From well-established names to newer entrants, the choices can be overwhelming. Begin by researching reputable brokerage platforms that align with your preferences, trading style, and financial goals.

Factors to Consider:
- Fees and Commissions: Compare the fees and commissions associated with different platforms. Some offer discounted rates for frequent traders or specific account types.
- Research Tools: Look for platforms that provide robust research tools. These tools can be invaluable for analyzing stocks, understanding market trends, and making informed decisions.
- User Interface: A user-friendly interface is crucial, especially for beginners. Explore platforms with intuitive designs that facilitate seamless navigation.

Customer Support: Consider the quality of customer support. A responsive and helpful support team can be a lifeline, particularly during your initial foray into trading.

Account Setup

Opening Your Trading Account:
Once you've selected a brokerage platform, the next step is opening a trading account. This involves providing personal and financial information, akin to setting up a bank account. The broker will guide you through this process, ensuring that you meet all necessary requirements.
Documentation Needed:
Be prepared to provide identification documents, proof of address, and other relevant paperwork. This is a standard procedure to comply with regulatory requirements.
Funding Your Account:
After your account is set up, you'll need to fund it. Most brokers offer various methods, including bank transfers and online payment gateways. Determine the funding method that suits you best, keeping in mind any associated fees or processing times.
Demo Accounts for Practice:
Many brokerage platforms also offer demo accounts. These simulate real-market conditions, allowing you to practice trading without risking real money. Take advantage of this invaluable resource to familiarize yourself with the platform and hone your trading skills.

Your First Trade

Understanding Order Types:
As you gear up for your inaugural trade, acquaint yourself with different order types. Market orders, limit orders, and stop orders are common types that influence how and when your trades are executed.
Start Small, Learn Big:
Consider making your initial trades with a smaller investment. This allows you to grasp the mechanics of buying and selling without exposing yourself to significant risk. As you gain confidence and experience, you can gradually increase your investment.

Conclusion

Congratulations! You've successfully set the stage for your stock market journey. In the next chapter, we'll explore the diverse landscape of investments, from individual stocks to bonds and mutual funds. As you venture into the exciting realm of trading, remember that learning is a continuous process. Embrace each step, and soon you'll be navigating the Indian stock market with confidence.
Happy trading, and may your investments flourish!

Chapter 3: Types of Investments

Welcome to the diverse world of investments! In this chapter, we'll embark on a journey to understand the different vehicles available in the stock market. From individual stocks to bonds and mutual funds, each investment type offers a unique opportunity for growth and financial success.

Individual Stocks

Owning a Piece of the Puzzle:
Investing in individual stocks means becoming a partial owner of a specific company. Whether it's a well-established giant or an up-and-coming star, owning shares in a company allows you to share in its successes and potentially benefit from its growth.
Research is Key:
Before diving into the stock market, take the time to research and analyze individual companies. Understand their financial health, growth prospects, and the industry they operate in. This knowledge is essential for making informed investment decisions.
Risk and Reward:
While individual stocks offer the potential for significant returns, they also come with higher risk. Prices can be volatile, and individual companies may face challenges. Diversification, a topic we'll explore in a later chapter, can help mitigate some of these risks.

Bonds

Steady Income with Bonds:
Bonds are debt securities where investors lend money to a company, municipality, or government in exchange for periodic interest payments and the return of the principal amount at maturity. Bonds are often considered safer than stocks and provide a steady income stream.
Understanding Bond Ratings:

Bonds come with credit ratings that indicate the issuer's creditworthiness. Ratings range from AAA (considered very low risk) to D (in default). Higher-rated bonds generally offer lower interest rates, while lower-rated bonds offer higher potential returns but come with increased risk.
Balancing Risk and Income:
Bonds are an excellent way to balance the risk in your investment portfolio. They provide a stable foundation and can serve as a source of income, especially during periods of market volatility.

Mutual Funds

Diversification Simplified:
Mutual funds pool money from multiple investors to invest in a diversified portfolio of stocks, bonds, or other securities. They offer instant diversification, allowing you to spread your investment across various assets without having to individually manage each one.
Professional Management:
One of the key advantages of mutual funds is professional management. Fund managers make decisions on behalf of investors, selecting and managing the fund's investments based on its objectives. This can be especially beneficial for those who are new to investing.
Types of Mutual Funds:
There are various types of mutual funds, including equity funds, debt funds, and hybrid funds. Each has its own risk-return profile, so it's essential to choose funds that align with your financial goals and risk tolerance.

Choosing the Right Mix

Building Your Portfolio:
As you embark on your investment journey, consider building a well-balanced portfolio that includes a mix of individual stocks, bonds, and mutual funds. The right combination depends on your financial goals, risk tolerance, and investment horizon.

Chapter 4: Fundamental Analysis

Welcome to the heart of stock market exploration! In this chapter, we'll unravel the art and science of fundamental analysis. This powerful tool allows investors to peek beneath the surface of individual companies, assessing their financial health and potential for future growth.

Understanding Fundamental Analysis
The Foundation of Informed Investing:
Fundamental analysis is like peeling back the layers of an onion. It involves a thorough examination of a company's financial statements, management, competitive position, and overall industry conditions. By understanding these factors, investors can make informed decisions about whether a particular stock is a sound investment.
Key Components of Fundamental Analysis:
Financial Statements:
- Balance Sheet: Provides a snapshot of a company's assets, liabilities, and equity at a specific point in time.
- Income Statement: Details a company's revenues, expenses, and profits over a set period.
- Cash Flow Statement: Tracks the flow of cash in and out of a company.

Earnings Per Share (EPS):
- EPS is a critical metric calculated by dividing a company's net income by its outstanding shares. It gives insights into a company's profitability on a per-share basis.

Price-to-Earnings (P/E) Ratio:
- The P/E ratio compares a company's stock price to its earnings per share. A high P/E ratio may indicate that the market expects strong future growth, while a low ratio may suggest undervaluation.

Dividend Yield:
- For income-oriented investors, the dividend yield measures the annual dividend income as a percentage of the stock's current price.

Evaluating a Company's Management

Leadership Matters:
A company's success often hinges on the effectiveness of its management team. Evaluate the track record and vision of the leadership, assessing whether their decisions align with the company's long-term goals.

Annual Reports and Investor Calls:
Dive into annual reports and listen to investor calls to gain insights into management's strategy, challenges, and plans for the future. Transparent and communicative leadership is a positive sign.

Assessing Competitive Position and Industry Conditions

Industry Analysis:
Consider the broader industry in which a company operates. Industry conditions can significantly impact a company's success. Analyze trends, potential disruptions, and the competitive landscape.

Competitive Advantage:
Identify a company's competitive advantages or unique selling points. Companies with a moat — a sustainable competitive advantage — are often better positioned for long-term success.

Putting It All Together

Creating a Holistic Picture:
Effective fundamental analysis involves synthesizing information from various sources to create a holistic view of a company. Consider how macroeconomic factors, industry trends, and company-specific factors interact.

Risks and Limitations:
Acknowledge that fundamental analysis has its limitations. External factors, unforeseen events, and market sentiment can impact stock prices. Diversification and a long-term perspective are essential risk management strategies.

Real-World Application

Case Studies and Practical Exercises:
To reinforce your understanding of fundamental analysis, this chapter includes case studies and practical exercises. Apply the concepts you've learned to real-world examples, honing your analytical skills.

Chapter 5: Technical Analysis

Welcome to the exciting realm of technical analysis! In this chapter, we'll uncover the art of reading stock charts, recognizing patterns, and utilizing technical indicators. These tools will empower you to make informed trading decisions based on historical price movements and market psychology.

The Basics of Technical Analysis

The Language of Charts:
At its core, technical analysis is about studying historical price and volume data to predict future price movements. Charts are the primary tool in this analysis, providing a visual representation of a stock's performance over time.
Common Chart Types:
- Line Charts: Display the closing prices over a specific period.
- Bar Charts: Illustrate opening, closing, high, and low prices for a given time frame.
- Candlestick Charts: Offer a visual representation of price movements, revealing market sentiment and trends.

Understanding Various Types of Charts

Welcome to the dynamic realm of chart analysis. Before delving into the intricate world of chart patterns, it's crucial to grasp the different types of charts that serve as the foundation of technical analysis. Each chart type presents information in a unique way, allowing traders to interpret market dynamics. Let's explore the various types of charts:

1. Line Chart:

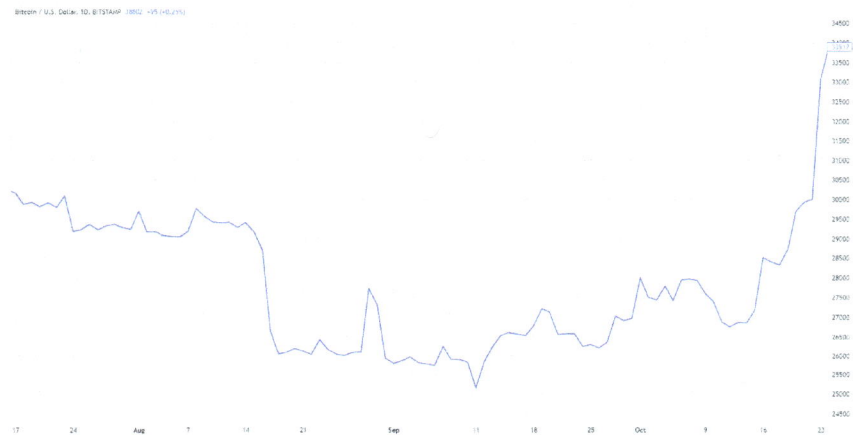

- Description: The line chart is the most straightforward, depicting the closing prices of an asset over a specific time frame. Connecting these closing prices creates a line that provides a clear visualization of the overall price trend.
- Use a Quick overview of trend direction and general price movements.

2. Bar Chart:

- Description: Bar charts illustrate the high, low, open, and close prices for a given time period using vertical bars. The opening price is represented by a horizontal line to the left, and the closing price by a line to the right.
- Use: Detailed representation of price movements and volatility.

3. Candlestick Chart:

- Description: Similar to bar charts, candlestick charts display open, high, low, and close prices. The body of each candlestick visually represents the price range between the open and close, with different colors indicating bullish (upward) or bearish (downward) movements.
- Use: Comprehensive analysis of market sentiment and potential trend reversals.

The Blueprint for Trend Line Trading Success

Embarking on the journey of precision trading involves harnessing the power of trend lines, indispensable tools for interpreting market trends. In this subchapter, we'll delve into the step-by-step process of effectively trading with trend lines to enhance your decision-making prowess.

Step 1: Deciphering the Trend

Identify the prevailing market trend by scrutinizing price charts. Distinguish between bullish, bearish, or range-bound conditions. Utilize indicators or visual analysis to validate the trend's direction.

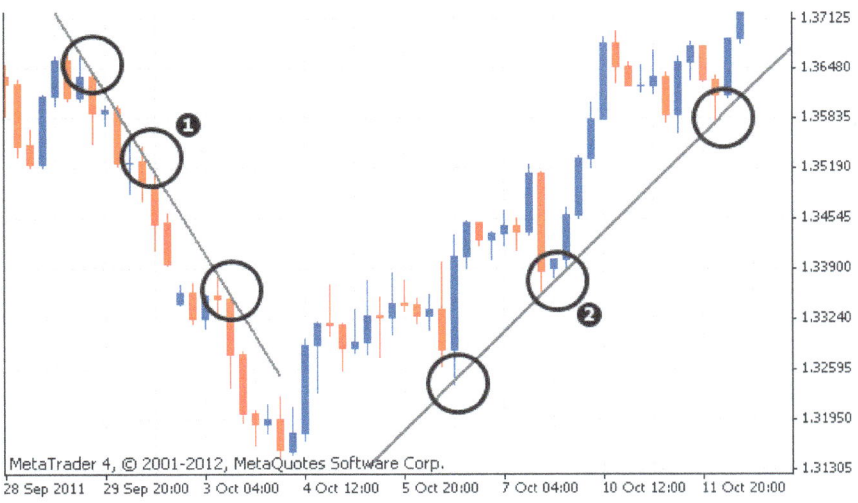

Step 2: Laying the Foundation

Draw trend lines beneath higher lows for an upward trend or above lower highs for a downward trend. In a sideways trend, create horizontal lines connecting peaks and troughs. Establish a foundation that captures the essence of the trend.

Step 3: Validation Check

Confirm the robustness of your trend lines by ensuring they align with multiple touchpoints. A trend line gains strength with each touchpoint, enhancing its reliability.

Step 4: Strategic Entry Points

- In a Bullish Trend:
- Identify opportunities for long positions when the price approaches the trend line after a pullback. Employ additional analysis, such as candlestick patterns or indicators, to confirm entry signals.
- In a Bearish Trend:
- Identify opportunities for short positions when the price approaches the trend line after a retracement. Confirm entry signals using complementary technical analysis tools.

Step 5: Risk Management

- Set stop-loss orders below the trend line for long positions and above the trend line for short positions. This prudent step helps mitigate risks in the event of unexpected price reversals.

Step 6: Targeting Profits

- Establish profit targets based on key support and resistance levels, chart patterns, or the projected distance of the expected price move. Use these targets to guide your take-profit decisions.

Step 7: Vigilance and Adjustment

- Monitor price action closely and observe the behavior of the trend line. Be alert to signs of potential reversals or weakening trends. Adjust the trend lines as needed to accommodate new price data.

Step 8: Synergizing Analysis Tools

- Enhance your trend line analysis by incorporating additional technical indicators, oscillators, or chart patterns. A holistic approach strengthens your trading strategy.

Step 9: Risk Management Practices

- Implement effective risk management strategies by avoiding excessive risk on individual trades. Never risk more than a predetermined percentage of your trading capital.

Step 10: Post-Trade Evaluation

- After the trade concludes, conduct a thorough evaluation. Analyze what contributed to success and identify areas for improvement. Use this feedback loop to refine and optimize your trading strategy.

By following this comprehensive blueprint, you'll be equipped to navigate the intricate world of trend line trading with precision and confidence. Your ability to interpret and leverage market trends will serve as a cornerstone for strategic decision-making in your trading journey.

Support:

Support is a price level at which a financial asset tends to stop falling and may even bounce back upwards. It acts as a metaphorical floor, preventing the price from declining further. Traders and investors often observe support levels to identify potential buying opportunities.

Characteristics:

Price Bounces: When the price approaches a support level, there is a tendency for buying interest to increase, leading to a bounce in the price.

Historical Significance: Support levels are often formed at previous areas where the price had experienced resistance or consolidation.
Psychological Impact: Support levels can also be psychological levels where traders expect buying interest to emerge.

Types of Support:

Horizontal Support: Occurs at a specific price level, forming a horizontal line on the chart.
Trendline Support: Forms along an upward-sloping trendline in an uptrend.

How to Identify Support:

Chart Patterns: Look for areas where the price has historically reversed or consolidated.
Moving Averages: Moving averages can act as dynamic support levels.
Volume Analysis: High trading volumes at a particular price level can indicate strong support.

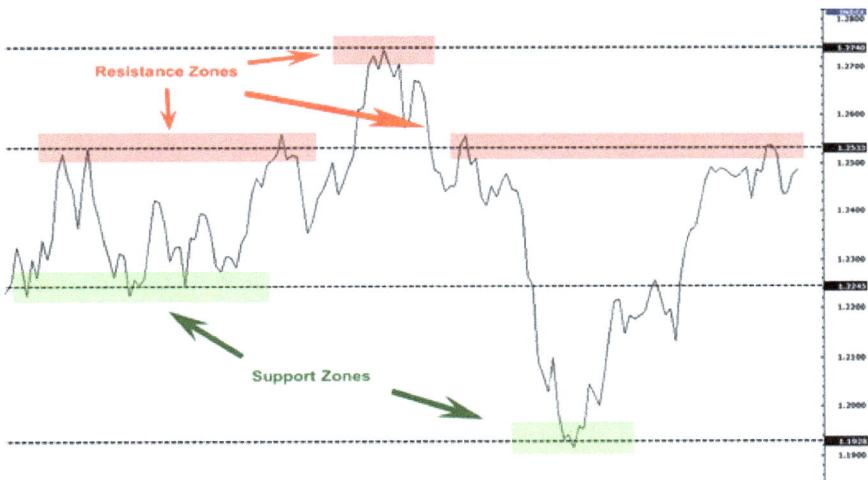

Resistance:

Definition:
Resistance is a price level at which a financial asset tends to stop rising and may face selling pressure, preventing the price from moving higher. It acts as a metaphorical ceiling, signaling a potential reversal or consolidation. Traders and investors watch resistance levels for potential selling or shorting opportunities.

Characteristics:

Price Reversals: When the price approaches a resistance level, selling interest tends to increase, leading to a potential reversal or a temporary halt in upward momentum.
Historical Significance: Resistance levels often form at previous areas where the price had faced support or consolidation.
Psychological Impact: Round numbers or significant price levels can act as psychological resistance.

Types of Resistance:

Horizontal Resistance: Occurs at a specific price level, forming a horizontal line on the chart.
Trendline Resistance: Forms along a downward-sloping trendline in a downtrend.

How to Identify Resistance:

Chart Patterns: Look for areas where the price has historically reversed or faced consolidation.
Fibonacci Levels: Fibonacci retracement levels can act as resistance levels.
Moving Averages: Moving averages can act as dynamic resistance levels.

Key Points:

Role Reversal: Once a support level is breached, it may turn into resistance, and vice versa.
Strength in Numbers: The more times a level is tested and holds, the stronger it becomes.
Confirmation: Use additional technical indicators or chart patterns to confirm the significance of support or resistance levels.
Dynamic Nature: Support and resistance levels can change over time as market dynamics evolve.

Chapter 6: Candlestick Chronicles: Unraveling Market Dynamics

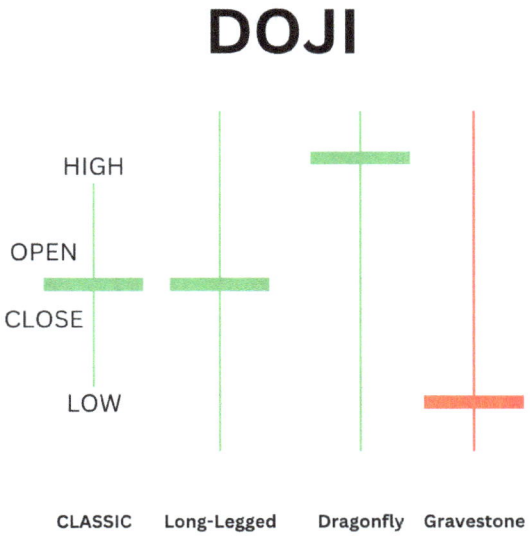

A Doji is a single candlestick pattern that reflects market indecision. It is formed when the opening and closing prices are very close or identical, resulting in a small or non-existent real body. The unique characteristic of a Doji is that it represents a temporary equilibrium between buyers and sellers, suggesting a tug-of-war between opposing market forces.

Here are the key components of a Doji:

Open and Close: The open and close prices are nearly the same, creating a small or non-existent real body. In some cases, the open and close prices might be identical, resulting in a horizontal line.

Upper and Lower Shadows: Dojis typically have upper and lower shadows, indicating the price range during the candle's time period. The length of these shadows can vary.

Market Indecision: The Doji's formation signifies uncertainty and indecision among market participants. Neither bulls nor bears have a clear advantage during the Doji period.

Potential Reversal or Continuation: While a Doji alone does not provide a clear directional signal, its appearance amid a prevailing trend can suggest a potential reversal or continuation, depending on the context.

There are variations of the Doji pattern that convey additional information about market sentiment:
- Long-Legged Doji: This type of Doji has longer upper and lower shadows, indicating higher volatility and more significant indecision.
- Dragonfly Doji: Characterized by a long lower shadow and a small or non-existent upper shadow, the Dragonfly Doji suggests that sellers dominated early in the trading session, but buyers managed to bring the price back up.
- Gravestone Doji: The Gravestone Doji has a long upper shadow and a small or non-existent lower shadow, indicating that buyers pushed the price higher during the session, but sellers regained control by the close.

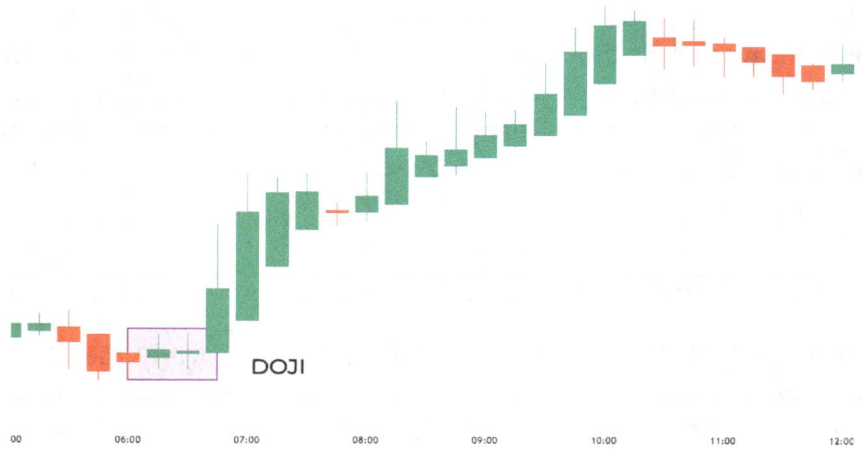

Interpretation of Doji Patterns:

Potential Reversal: A Doji appearing after a prolonged uptrend may signal the potential exhaustion of bullish momentum and a reversal. Similarly, a Doji following a downtrend might suggest a potential bullish reversal.

Market Consolidation: In a sideways or ranging market, Dojis can indicate continued market indecision and consolidation.

Confirmation Needed: Traders often seek confirmation from subsequent price action, such as a bullish or bearish candle, to validate the potential reversal signaled by the Doji.

Context Matters: The effectiveness of a Doji depends on its position within the broader trend and the overall market conditions. Consider the context, such as support/resistance levels or trendlines, for a more accurate analysis.

While Dojis can be informative, they are most powerful when used in conjunction with other technical indicators and chart patterns. Traders often incorporate Doji patterns into their overall analysis to refine entry and exit points in the market.

HAMMER

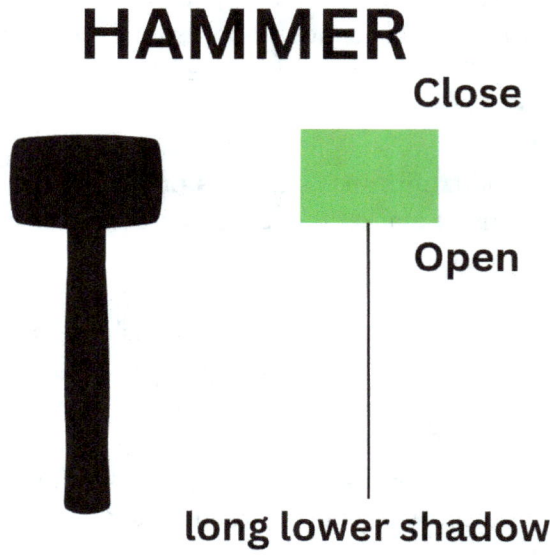

The Hammer is a single candlestick pattern that typically occurs at the end of a downtrend and signals a potential bullish reversal. It's characterized by a small real body near the top of the candle, a long lower shadow (tail), and little to no upper shadow. The shape of the candle resembles a hammer, with a small body and a long handle. Here are the key components and the interpretation of the Hammer pattern:

Characteristics of a Hammer:

Small Real Body:

- The real body of the candle is small and positioned at the upper end of the candlestick.

- Long Lower Shadow (Tail):
- The most distinctive feature is a long lower shadow that extends below the real body. This represents the distance between the low and the opening or closing price.
- Little to No Upper Shadow:
- The upper shadow is either very small or non-existent, indicating that the closing price is near the high of the session.

Starting at the far left of the price chart, we can see that the price action here has been carving out a downtrend. After some period of consolidation and a minor upside retracement, prices resume their downward descent, and eventually, a bullish hammer candlestick pattern emerges. After the bullish hammer candle completes, a price reversal occurs in the market, and prices begin to rise steadily.

If you look closely at the bullish hammer within the circled area, you can see that this candle meets all of our required characteristics for a hammer formation. More specifically, notice how the length of the lower shadow is at least two-thirds of the entire formation. Additionally, you can see that the body of the hammer candle is relatively small and closes near the upper end of the range. Finally, notice the relatively small upper wick within this formation.

Interpretation of the Hammer Pattern:
Bullish Reversal Signal:
- The Hammer is a bullish reversal pattern, suggesting a potential change in the prevailing downtrend. It indicates that sellers were initially in control but lost their grip, allowing buyers to push the price higher.
- Strong Buying Interest: The long lower shadow indicates that there was significant buying interest at lower prices. The price moved well below the opening level but managed to recover by the end of the session.
- Confirmation Needed: Traders often look for confirmation in the form of a bullish candle on the following trading day. A bullish follow-up confirms the potential reversal signaled by the Hammer.
- Support and Resistance Considerations: Hammers are often more significant when they appear near key support levels or trendlines, adding weight to the potential reversal scenario.

SHOOTING STAR

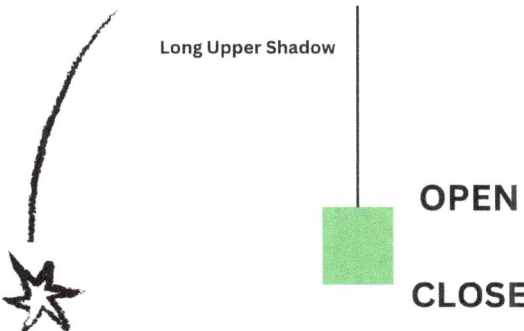

The Shooting Star is a single candlestick pattern that occurs at the end of an uptrend and signals a potential bearish reversal. It has a small real body near the bottom of the candle, a long upper shadow, and little to no lower shadow. The appearance of the candlestick is reminiscent of a shooting star, with a small body and an elongated tail pointing upwards.

Here are the key components and the interpretation of the Shooting Star pattern:

Characteristics of a Shooting Star:

- Small Real Body: The real body of the candle is small and positioned at the lower end of the candlestick.
- Long Upper Shadow: The most prominent feature is a long upper shadow that extends above the real body. This represents the distance between the high and the opening or closing price

- Little to No Lower Shadow: The lower shadow is either very small or non-existent, indicating that the closing price is near the low of the session.

Interpretation of the Shooting Star Pattern:

- Bearish Reversal Signal: The Shooting Star is a bearish reversal pattern, suggesting a potential change in the prevailing uptrend. It indicates that buyers were initially in control but lost momentum, allowing sellers to push the price lower.
- Strong Selling Pressure: The long upper shadow indicates that there was significant selling pressure at higher prices. The price moved well above the opening level but couldn't sustain those higher levels.
- Confirmation Needed: Traders often look for confirmation in the form of a bearish candle on the following trading day. A bearish follow-up confirms the potential reversal signaled by the Shooting Star.
- Resistance Considerations: Shooting Stars are often more significant when they appear near key resistance levels or trendlines, adding weight to the potential reversal scenario.

Engulfing Pattern

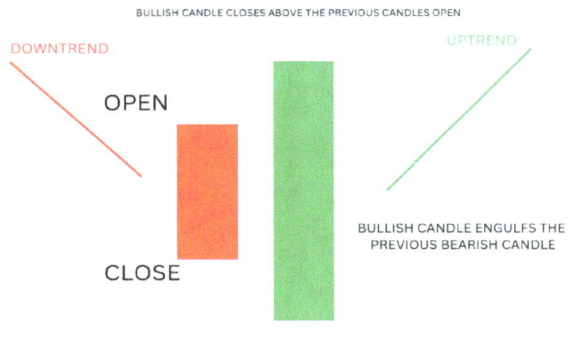

Engulfing patterns are candlestick patterns that consist of two candles and are indicative of potential trend reversals. There are two types of engulfing patterns: bullish engulfing and bearish engulfing.

1. Bullish Engulfing Pattern:
- Description: The bullish engulfing pattern occurs during a downtrend and consists of two candles. The first candle is a bearish (downward) candle, followed by a larger bullish (upward) candle. The second candle completely engulfs the body of the first candle, meaning it opens below the close of the first candle and closes above the opening of the first candle.
- Interpretation: The bullish engulfing pattern is a strong signal of potential bullish reversal. It suggests that after a period of selling pressure, buyers have gained control, leading to a shift in sentiment. The larger bullish candle indicates strong buying interest and the potential for a new uptrend.

2. Bearish Engulfing Pattern:
- Description: The bearish engulfing pattern occurs during an uptrend and also consists of two candles. The first candle is a bullish (upward) candle, followed by a larger bearish (downward) candle. The second candle completely engulfs the body of the first candle, opening above the close of the first candle and closing below the open of the first candle.
- Interpretation: The bearish engulfing pattern is a strong signal of potential bearish reversal. It suggests that after a period of buying activity, sellers have gained control, leading to a shift in sentiment. The larger bearish candle indicates strong selling interest and the potential for a new downtrend.

Considerations for Engulfing Patterns:

- Size Matters: The larger the second candle in the engulfing pattern, the more significant the reversal signal. It indicates stronger momentum in the new direction.
- Volume Confirmation: Traders often look for confirmation through higher trading volumes during the engulfing pattern. Higher volumes add validity to the strength of the reversal.
- Contextual Analysis: Engulfing patterns are more potent when they occur at significant support or resistance levels, adding confluence to the reversal signal.

- Confirmation Candle: Traders often seek confirmation from subsequent price action to ensure the validity of the reversal. A follow-up candle in the direction of the engulfing pattern adds confirmation.
- As with any technical analysis tool, it's crucial to use engulfing patterns in conjunction with other indicators and chart patterns for a comprehensive understanding of market dynamics. Additionally, considering the broader market context enhances the reliability of these reversal signals.

Morning Star

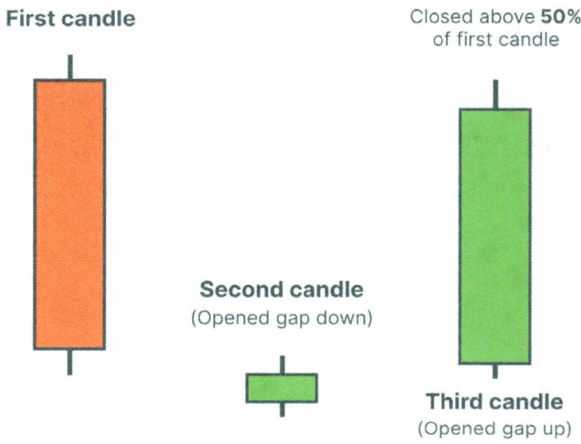

The Morning Star is a bullish reversal candlestick pattern that typically occurs at the end of a downtrend. It is composed of three candles and signifies a potential shift in market sentiment from bearish to bullish. The pattern is considered a strong indication that buyers are gaining control after a period of selling pressure.
Characteristics of the Morning Star Pattern:
First Candle (Bearish):
- The pattern begins with a large bearish (downward) candle, indicating a continuation of the existing downtrend.
- Second Candle (Indecisive or Small): The second candle is often smaller and has a small real body. It represents a period of indecision and a potential slowing down of the selling pressure. This candle can be bullish, bearish, or a doji.
- Third Candle (Bullish): The third candle is a large bullish (upward) candle that closes well above the midpoint of the first bearish candle. This bullish candle indicates a strong shift in

sentiment, with buyers taking control.

Interpretation of the Morning Star Pattern:
- Bullish Reversal Signal: The Morning Star is a strong signal of a potential bullish reversal. It suggests that after a prolonged downtrend, buyers are stepping in, and a new uptrend may be emerging.
- Confirmation Needed: While the Morning Star pattern is powerful on its own, traders often seek confirmation from subsequent price action. A follow-up bullish candle or other bullish signals strengthen the confidence in the reversal.
- Volume Consideration: Higher trading volumes during the formation of the Morning Star add weight to the reversal signal, indicating increased buying interest.
- Support and Resistance Levels: The effectiveness of the Morning Star is enhanced when it forms near key support levels or trendlines, adding confluence to the potential reversal scenario.

EVENING STAR

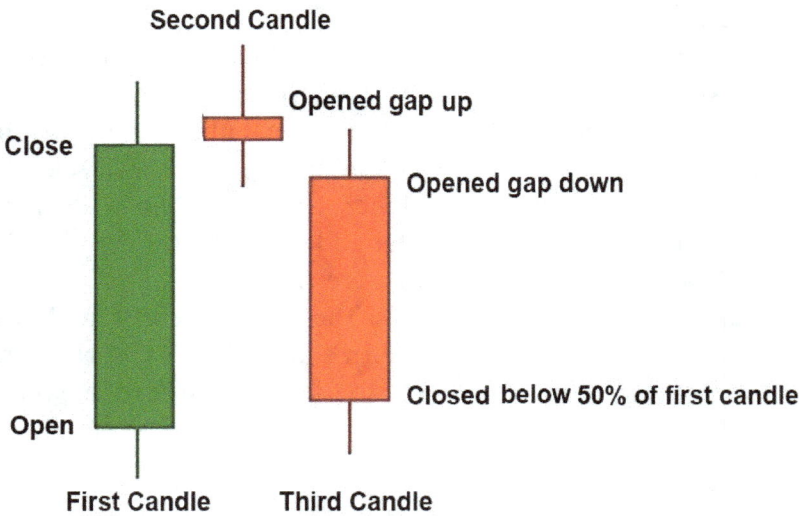

The Evening Star is a bearish reversal candlestick pattern that typically forms at the end of an uptrend. It consists of three candles and signals a potential shift in market sentiment from bullish to bearish. The Evening Star pattern is the opposite of the Morning Star pattern, representing a transition from optimism to pessimism among market participants.

Characteristics of the Evening Star Pattern:

- First Candle (Bullish): The pattern begins with a large bullish (upward) candle, indicating a strong uptrend.
- Second Candle (Indecisive or Small): The second candle is often smaller and has a small real body. It represents a period of indecision and a potential slowing down of the bullish momentum. This candle can be bullish, bearish, or a doji.

- Third Candle (Bearish): The third candle is a large bearish (downward) candle that closes well below the midpoint of the first bullish candle. This bearish candle indicates a strong shift in sentiment, with sellers gaining control.
- Interpretation of the Evening Star Pattern: Bearish Reversal Signal: The Evening Star is a strong signal of a potential bearish reversal. It suggests that after a prolonged uptrend, sellers are stepping in, and a new downtrend may be emerging.
- Confirmation Needed: While the Evening Star pattern is powerful on its own, traders often seek confirmation from subsequent price action. A follow-up bearish candle or other bearish signals strengthen the confidence in the reversal.
- Volume Consideration: Higher trading volumes during the formation of the Evening Star add weight to the reversal signal, indicating increased selling interest.
- Support and Resistance Levels: The effectiveness of the Evening Star is enhanced when it forms near key resistance levels or trendlines, adding confluence to the potential reversal scenario.

BULLISH HARAMI

BEARISH HARAMI

The Harami is a candlestick pattern that consists of two candles and indicates a potential reversal or indecision in the market. The pattern can be bullish (bullish harami) or bearish (bearish harami), and it is considered a signal that the current trend may be losing momentum.

1. Bullish Harami:
- Description: The first candle is a large bearish (downward) candle, indicating a prevailing downtrend.
- The second candle is a smaller bullish (upward) candle that is completely contained within the range of the first candle. The body of the second candle is often referred to as being "engulfed" by the first candle.
- Interpretation: The bullish harami suggests that after a period of strong selling pressure, there is a potential weakening of bearish momentum. The smaller bullish candle indicates indecision, and it could be a sign that buyers are starting to step in.

2. Bearish Harami:
- Description: The first candle is a large bullish (upward) candle, indicating a prevailing uptrend.

- The second candle is a smaller bearish (downward) candle that is completely contained within the range of the first candle

Interpretation:
- The bearish harami suggests that after a period of strong buying activity, there is a potential weakening of bullish momentum. The smaller bearish candle indicates indecision, and it could be a sign that sellers are starting to gain control.
- Considerations for Trading with Harami Patterns:
- Confirmation: Traders often look for confirmation from subsequent price action after the harami pattern. A follow-up candle in the direction of the potential reversal strengthens the confidence in the signal.
- Volume Analysis: Higher trading volumes during the harami pattern formation can add validity to the potential reversal.
- Contextual Analysis: Consider the broader market context, such as support and resistance levels or trendlines, when interpreting harami patterns.
- Variations: There are variations of the harami pattern, such as the harami cross and the harami dragonfly/doji. These variations may have different implications for market direction.
- Harami patterns are versatile and can be used in various timeframes. As with any technical analysis tool, it's essential to use harami patterns in conjunction with other indicators and chart patterns for a more comprehensive understanding of market dynamics.

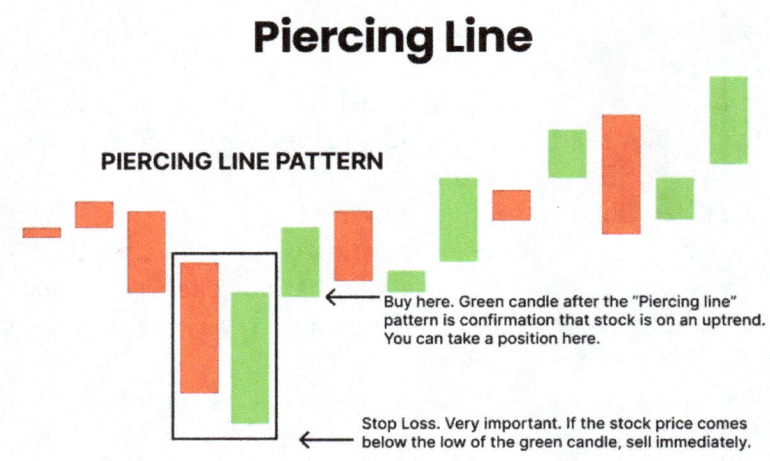

The Piercing Line is a bullish reversal candlestick pattern that forms during a downtrend. It consists of two candles and suggests a potential shift in market sentiment from bearish to bullish. The pattern indicates that buyers are gaining strength after a period of selling pressure.

Characteristics of the Piercing Line Pattern:

First Candle (Bearish):

- The pattern begins with a large bearish (downward) candle, indicating a prevailing downtrend.

Second Candle (Bullish):

- The second candle is a bullish (upward) candle that opens below the close of the first bearish candle but closes well into the body of the first candle. The closing price of the second candle is significantly higher than the midpoint of the first candle.
- Interpretation of the Piercing Line Pattern:
- Bullish Reversal Signal: The Piercing Line is a strong signal of a potential bullish reversal. It suggests that after a period of strong selling pressure, buyers are stepping in, causing the price to bounce back.
- Confirmation Needed: While the Piercing Line pattern is powerful on its own, traders often seek confirmation from

subsequent price action. A follow-up bullish candle or other bullish signals strengthen the confidence in the reversal.
- Volume Consideration: Higher trading volumes during the formation of the Piercing Line add weight to the reversal signal, indicating increased buying interest.
- Support Levels: The effectiveness of the Piercing Line is enhanced when it forms near key support levels or trendlines, adding confluence to the potential reversal scenario.

Dark Cloud Cover

The Dark Cloud Cover is a bearish reversal candlestick pattern that forms during an uptrend. It consists of two candles and suggests a potential shift in market sentiment from bullish to bearish. The pattern indicates that sellers are gaining strength after a period of buying activity.

Characteristics of the Dark Cloud Cover Pattern:
- First Candle (Bullish): The pattern begins with a large bullish (upward) candle, indicating a prevailing uptrend.
- Second Candle (Bearish): The second candle is a bearish (downward) candle that opens above the close of the first bullish candle but closes well into the body of the first candle. The closing price of the second candle is significantly below the midpoint of the first candle.
- Interpretation of the Dark Cloud Cover Pattern:
- Bearish Reversal Signal: The Dark Cloud Cover is a strong signal of a potential bearish reversal. It suggests that after a period of strong buying activity, sellers are stepping in, causing the price to pull back.
- Confirmation Needed: While the Dark Cloud Cover pattern is powerful on its own, traders often seek confirmation from subsequent price action. A follow-up bearish candle or other

bearish signals strengthen the confidence in the reversal.
- Volume Consideration: Higher trading volumes during the formation of the Dark Cloud Cover add weight to the reversal signal, indicating increased selling interest.
- Resistance Levels: The effectiveness of the Dark Cloud Cover is enhanced when it forms near key resistance levels or trendlines, adding confluence to the potential reversal scenario.

THREE INSIDE UP CANDLESTICK

The Three Inside Up is a bullish reversal candlestick pattern that forms during a downtrend. It consists of three candles and suggests a potential shift in market sentiment from bearish to bullish. The pattern indicates that buyers are gaining control after a period of selling pressure.

Characteristics of the Three Inside Up Pattern:
- First Candle (Bearish): The pattern begins with a large bearish (downward) candle, indicating a prevailing downtrend.
- Second Candle (Bullish): The second candle is a smaller bullish (upward) candle that is completely contained within the range of the first bearish candle.
- Third Candle (Bullish): The third candle is a large bullish (upward) candle that closes above the high of the first bearish candle, essentially engulfing both the first and second candles

Interpretation of the Three Inside Up Pattern:
- Bullish Reversal Signal: The Three Inside Up is a strong signal of a potential bullish reversal. It suggests that after a period of strong selling pressure, buyers are stepping in, causing the price to rebound.
- Confirmation Needed: While the Three Inside Up pattern is

powerful on its own, traders often seek confirmation from subsequent price action. A follow-up bullish candle or other bullish signals strengthen the confidence in the reversal.
- Volume Consideration: Higher trading volumes during the formation of the Three Inside Up add weight to the reversal signal, indicating increased buying interest.
- Support Levels: The effectiveness of the Three Inside Up is enhanced when it forms near key support levels or trendlines, adding confluence to the potential reversal scenario.

Chapter 7: Mastering Breakout Patterns: Unleashing Market Momentum

Double Top Formation

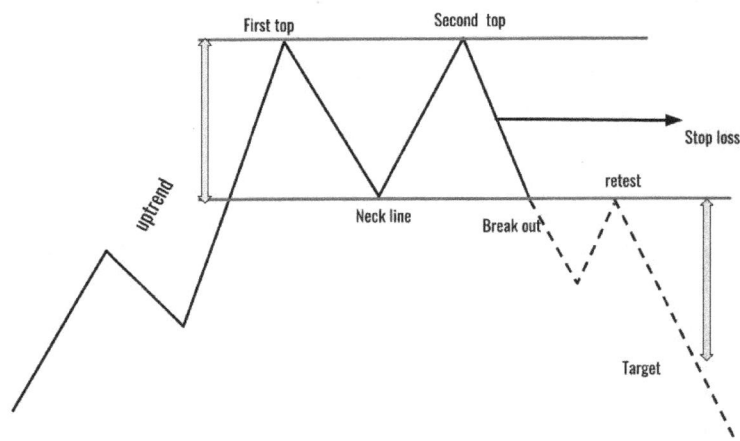

The double top breakout pattern is a common chart pattern used in technical analysis to identify potential reversals in an uptrend. Here's a detailed explanation of the double top breakout pattern:

Double Top Formation
1. Definition: The double top pattern forms after an extended uptrend and consists of two peaks (or tops) that reach a similar high, separated by a trough (or valley) in between.

2. Characteristics:
   - The first peak (top) is formed when the price reaches a certain level and then retraces.
   - The price then rallies again to a similar high (or slightly lower high), forming the second peak.

- The trough (valley) between the two peaks represents a level of support.

3. Key Elements:
   - Peaks: The two peaks should be relatively close in height and visually resemble two tops on the price chart.
   - Trough: The trough (valley) between the peaks acts as a support level. If this support level is breached, it signals a potential breakout.

Breakout Trigger
- Confirmation: The breakout occurs when the price decisively breaks below the trough (valley) that separates the two peaks.
- Volume: Ideally, the breakout should be accompanied by increased volume, indicating strong selling pressure and confirming the validity of the pattern.

Trading the Double Top Breakout
- Entry Point: Traders typically enter short positions (sell) when the price breaks below the trough (support level) that forms between the two peaks.
- Stop-Loss: Place a stop-loss order above the highest point of the double top pattern to manage risk.
- Target: The price target for this pattern is usually measured by projecting the distance from the trough to the highest peak below the breakout point.

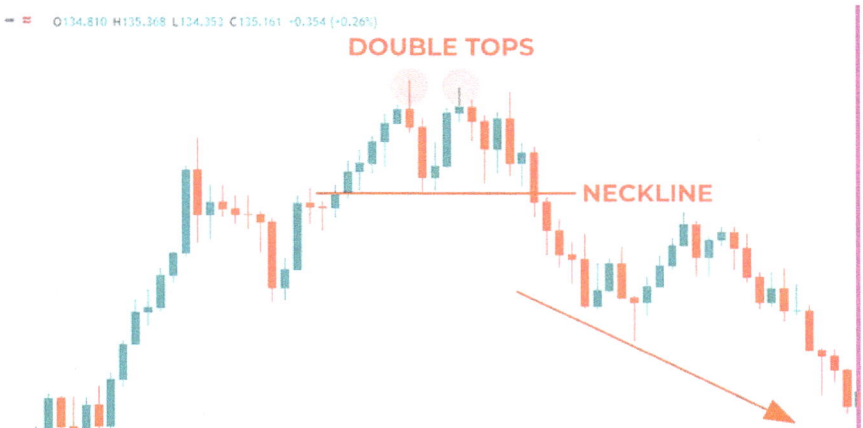

Double Bottom Pattern

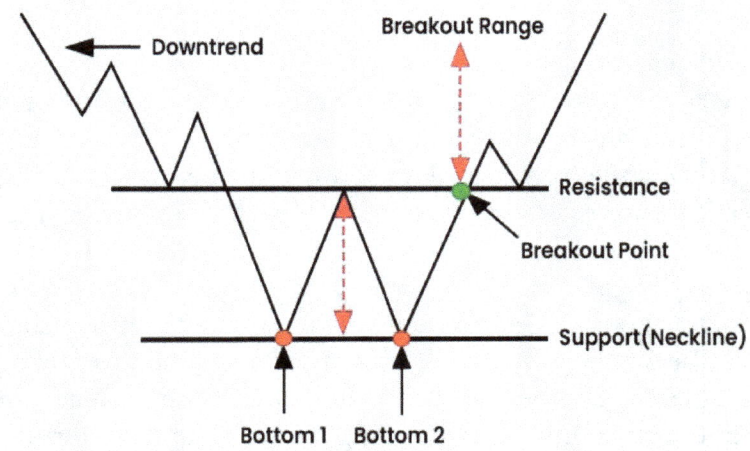

Double Top Chart Pattern

The double bottom pattern is a classic bullish reversal pattern used in technical analysis to identify potential buying opportunities after an extended downtrend. Here's an explanation of the double bottom pattern:

Double Bottom Formation
1. Definition: The double bottom pattern consists of two troughs (or bottoms) that reach a similar low, separated by a peak (or high) in between.

2. Characteristics:
   - The first trough (bottom) is formed when the price reaches a low point and then bounces back up.
   - The price then declines again to a similar low (or slightly higher low), forming the second trough.
   - The peak (high) between the two troughs acts as a resistance level.

3. Key Elements:
   - Troughs: The two troughs should be relatively close in depth and

visually resemble two bottoms on the price chart.
- Peak: The peak (high) between the troughs acts as a resistance level. A breakout above this resistance confirms the pattern.

Breakout Trigger
Confirmation: The breakout occurs when the price decisively breaks above the peak (high) that separates the two troughs.
- Volume: Ideally, the breakout should be accompanied by increased volume, indicating strong buying interest and confirming the validity of the pattern.

Trading the Double Bottom Breakout
- Entry Point: Traders typically enter long positions (buy) when the price breaks above the peak (resistance level) that forms between the two troughs.
- Stop-Loss: Place a stop-loss order below the lowest point of the double bottom pattern to manage risk.
- Target: The price target for this pattern is usually measured by projecting the distance from the peak to the lowest trough above the breakout point.

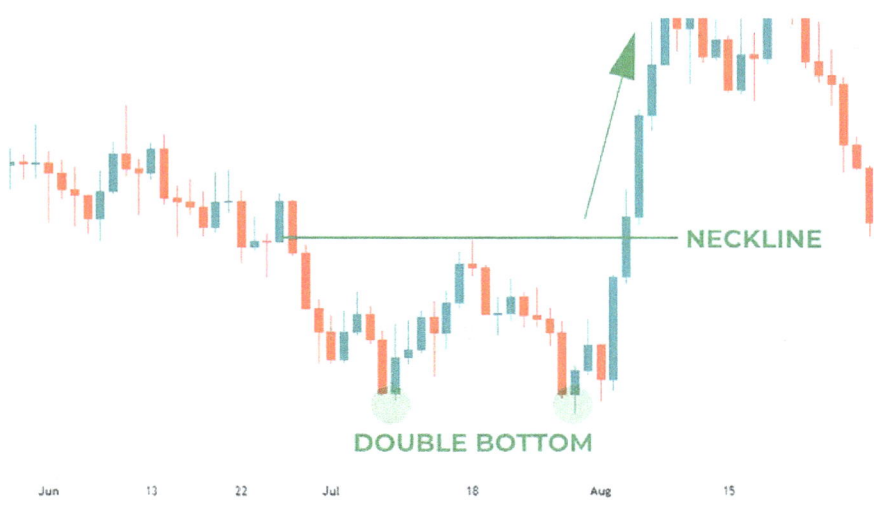

Triple Top Pattern

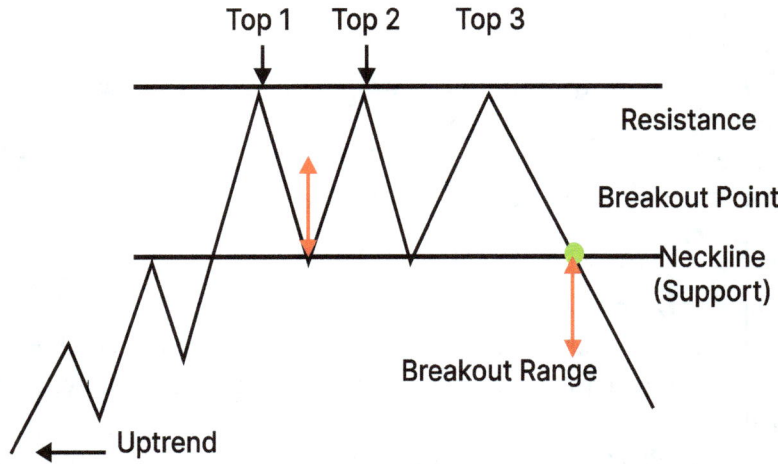

The triple top pattern is a bearish reversal pattern seen in technical analysis, indicating a potential trend reversal from an uptrend to a downtrend. Here's a detailed explanation of the triple top pattern:

Triple Top Formation
1. Definition: The triple top pattern consists of three consecutive peaks (or tops) that reach a similar high, separated by two intermittent troughs (or valleys) in between.

2. Characteristics:
   - The price reaches a peak and then retraces, forming the first top.
   - After a decline, the price rallies again to approximately the same high, forming the second top.
   - Following another decline, the price rallies once more to a similar high or slightly lower high, forming the third top.
   - The intermittent troughs (valleys) between the tops act as support levels.

3. Key Elements:
   - Peaks: The three peaks should be relatively close in height and visually resemble three tops on the price chart.

- Troughs: The troughs (valleys) between the tops represent support levels where buying interest temporarily halts the decline.

Breakout Trigger
- Confirmation: The breakout occurs when the price decisively breaks below the support level formed by the two intervening troughs (valleys) between the tops.
- Volume: Ideally, the breakout should be accompanied by increased volume, indicating strong selling pressure and confirming the validity of the pattern.

Trading the Triple Top Breakout
- Entry Point: Traders typically enter short positions (sell) when the price breaks below the support level that connects the two troughs (valleys) between the triple tops.
- Stop-Loss: Place a stop-loss order above the highest peak of the triple top pattern to manage risk.
- Target: The price target for this pattern is usually measured by projecting the distance from the support level to the lowest low following the breakout.

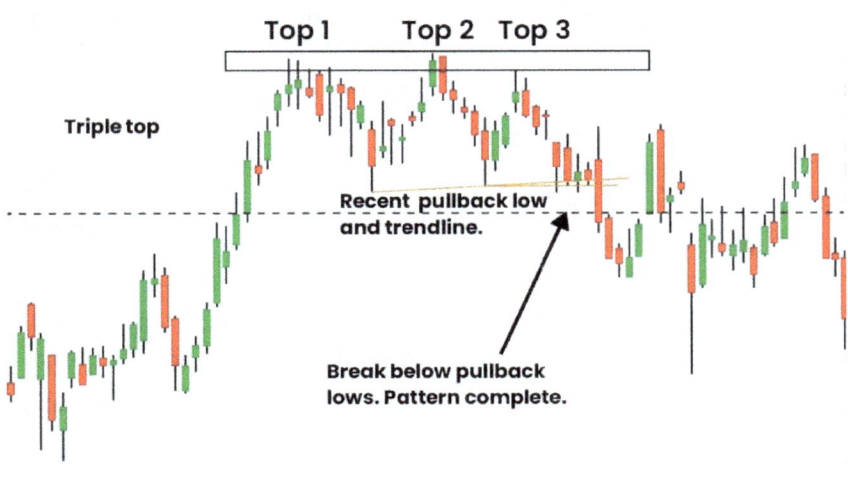

Tripple Bottom Pattern

The triple bottom pattern is a bullish reversal pattern observed in technical analysis, signaling a potential trend reversal from a downtrend to an uptrend. Here's an explanation of the triple bottom pattern:

Triple Bottom Formation
1. Definition: The triple bottom pattern consists of three consecutive troughs (or bottoms) that reach a similar low, separated by two intermittent peaks (or highs) in between.

2. Characteristics:
   - The price reaches a low and then bounces back up, forming the first bottom.
   - After a rally, the price declines again to approximately the same low, forming the second bottom.
   - Following another rally and subsequent decline, the price reaches a similar low or slightly higher low, forming the third bottom.
   - The intermittent peaks (highs) between the bottoms act as resistance levels.

3. Key Elements:
   -Bottoms: The three bottoms should be relatively close in depth and visually resemble three troughs on the price chart.
   - Peaks: The peaks (highs) between the bottoms represent resistance levels where selling pressure temporarily halts the ascent.

Breakout Trigger
- Confirmation: The breakout occurs when the price decisively breaks above the resistance level formed by the two intervening peaks (highs) between the triple bottoms.
- Volume: Ideally, the breakout should be accompanied by increased volume, indicating strong buying interest and confirming the validity of the pattern.

Trading the Triple Bottom Breakout
- Entry Point: Traders typically enter long positions (buy) when the price breaks above the resistance level that connects the two peaks (highs) between the triple bottoms.
- Stop-Loss: Place a stop-loss order below the lowest low of the triple bottom pattern to manage risk.
- Target: The price target for this pattern is usually measured by projecting the distance from the resistance level to the highest high following the breakout.

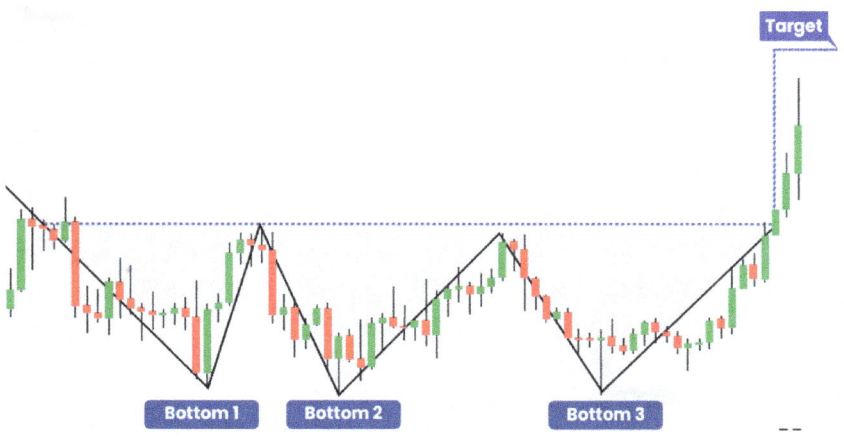

Head And Shoulders Pattern

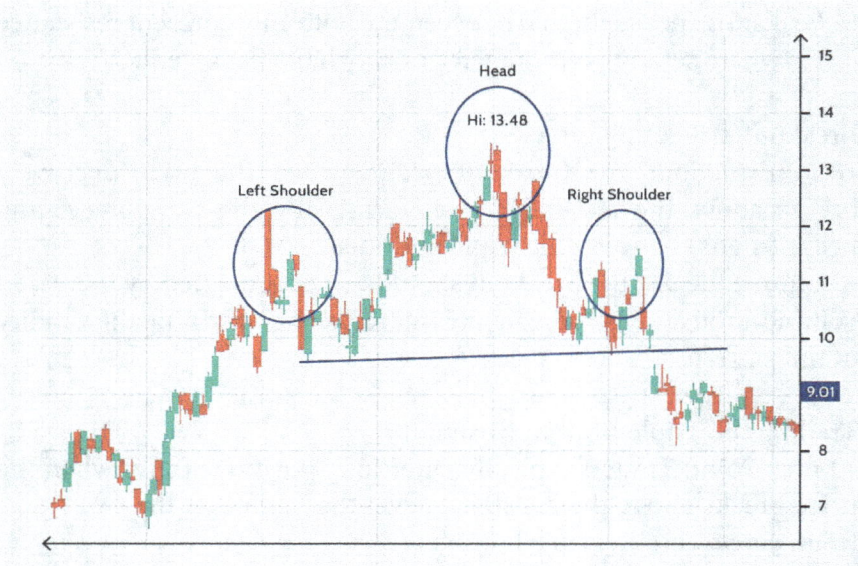

The head and shoulders pattern is a widely recognized and reliable trend reversal pattern in technical analysis. It is named for its appearance, which resembles a human head and shoulders, and it signals a shift from an uptrend to a potential downtrend. Here's a detailed explanation of the head and shoulders pattern:

Head and Shoulders Pattern Formation
1. Definition: The head and shoulders pattern consists of three peaks (or highs) with the middle peak (head) being the highest, separated by two lower peaks (shoulders) on either side.
2. Characteristics:
  - Left Shoulder: The first peak (shoulder) forms during an uptrend, followed by a retracement.
  - Head: The highest peak (head) forms next, signaling the peak of the uptrend.
  - Right Shoulder: Another peak (shoulder) forms after the head, usually lower than the head peak.
  - The troughs (lows) between the shoulders and the head act as support levels.

3. Key Elements:
 - Peaks (Highs): The three peaks create a distinctive visual pattern resembling the outline of a head and shoulders.
 - Neckline: A trendline drawn connecting the lows of the two troughs (valleys) can serve as the neckline of the pattern.

Head and Shoulders Breakdown
-Confirmation: The breakdown occurs when the price breaks below the neckline after forming the right shoulder.
- Volume: A breakout below the neckline should ideally be accompanied by increased volume, confirming the pattern's validity.

Trading the Head and Shoulders Pattern
- Entry Point: Traders typically enter short positions (sell) when the price breaks below the neckline after the formation of the right shoulder.
- Stop-Loss: Place a stop-loss order above the right shoulder's peak to manage risk.
- Target: The price target for this pattern is usually measured by projecting the distance from the head to the neckline below the breakout point.

Inverse Head and Shoulders

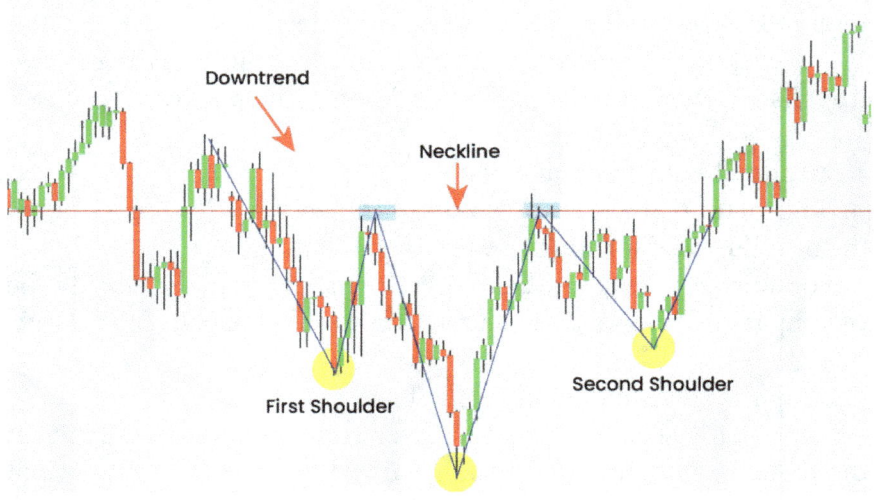

Inverse Head and Shoulders
- Conversely, an inverse head and shoulders pattern signals a bullish reversal:
    - Left Shoulder: The first trough (shoulder) forms during a downtrend, followed by a retracement.
    - Head: The lowest trough (head) forms next, signaling the lowest point of the downtrend.
    - Right Shoulder: Another trough (shoulder) forms after the head, usually higher than the head trough.
    - The peaks (highs) between the shoulders and the head act as resistance levels.

Example:
- Chart Analysis:
    - Identify the three distinctive peaks (or troughs for inverse head and shoulders) forming the pattern.
    - Draw a neckline connecting the lows (or highs for inverse) of the two shoulders.
    - Monitor the price for a breakout below (or above for inverse) the neckline with confirmation.

- Execution:
  - Enter a short trade (sell) when the price breaks below the neckline of a head and shoulders pattern.
  - Enter a long trade (buy) when the price breaks above the neckline of an inverse head and shoulders pattern.
  - Place a stop-loss order above the right shoulder's peak (or below for inverse).
  - Set a price target based on the pattern's projected move.

The head and shoulders pattern is a powerful tool for identifying potential trend reversals and can be used effectively in conjunction with other technical indicators and risk management strategies. Traders should wait for confirmation of the breakout and consider market conditions before entering a trade based on this pattern.

The Falling Wedge Pattern

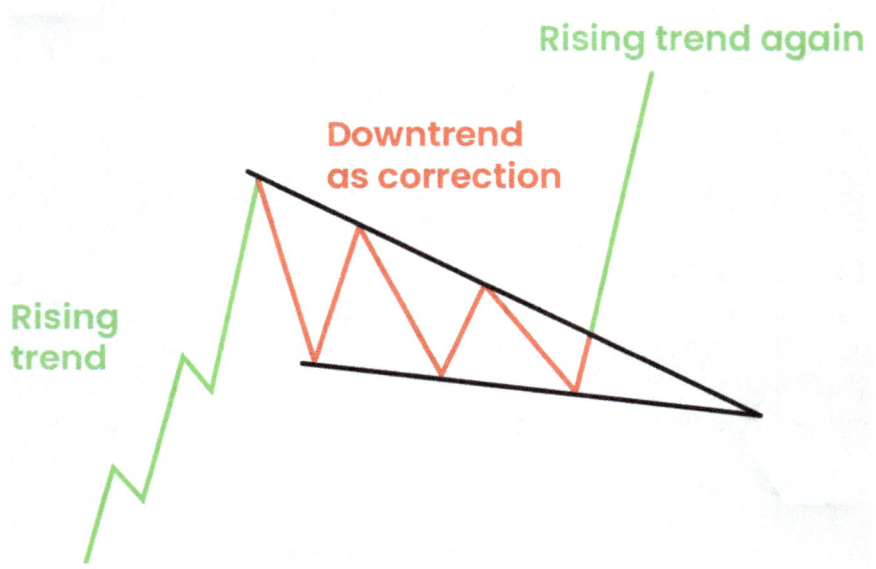

The falling wedge pattern is a bullish chart pattern characterized by converging trendlines that slope downward. It typically forms during a downtrend and signals a potential reversal or continuation of the current trend. Here's an explanation of the falling wedge pattern:

Falling Wedge Pattern Formation
1. Definition: The falling wedge pattern is formed by two downward-sloping trendlines that converge as they move lower. The upper trendline (resistance line) and the lower trendline (support line) both slope downward.

2. Characteristics:
   - Upper Trendline (Resistance): Connects the highs of the price action, sloping downward.
   - Lower Trendline (Support): Connects the lows of the price action, also sloping downward.
   - The price contracts within the narrowing range of the wedge, forming lower highs and lower lows.

Key Elements of the Falling Wedge Pattern
- Slope of Trendlines:
  - The upper resistance trendline should have a steeper slope than the lower support trendline.
  - The converging trendlines create a narrowing wedge shape.

Breakout and Trading the Falling Wedge Pattern
- Breakout Direction: The breakout from a falling wedge pattern is typically upward, signaling a bullish reversal.
- Confirmation: Look for a decisive breakout above the upper resistance trendline.
- Volume: Ideally, the breakout should be accompanied by an increase in volume, confirming the validity of the pattern.

Entry and Target Levels
- Entry Point: Traders often enter long positions (buy) upon the breakout above the upper trendline of the falling wedge pattern.
- Stop-Loss: Place a stop-loss order below the lower trendline of the wedge pattern to manage risk.
- Target: The price target is usually set based on the height of the wedge pattern, measured from the widest point of the wedge to the breakout point.

The Rising Wedge Pattern

Price broke down, dowtrend resumes...

The rising wedge pattern is a bearish chart pattern characterized by converging trendlines that slope upward. It typically forms during an uptrend and signals a potential reversal or continuation of the current trend. Here's an explanation of the rising wedge pattern:

Rising Wedge Pattern Formation
1. Definition: The rising wedge pattern is formed by two upward-sloping trendlines that converge as they move higher. The lower trendline (support line) and the upper trendline (resistance line) both slope upward.

2. Characteristics:
   - Lower Trendline (Support): Connects the lows of the price action, sloping upward.
   - Upper Trendline (Resistance): Connects the highs of the price action, also sloping upward.
   - The price contracts within the narrowing range of the wedge, forming higher highs and higher lows.

Key Elements of the Rising Wedge Pattern
- Slope of Trendlines:
  - The upper resistance trendline should have a shallower slope than the lower support trendline.
  - The converging trendlines create a narrowing wedge shape.

Breakdown and Trading the Rising Wedge Pattern
- Breakdown Direction: The breakdown from a rising wedge pattern is typically downward, signaling a bearish reversal.
- Confirmation: Look for a decisive breakdown below the lower support trendline.
- Volume: Ideally, the breakdown should be accompanied by an increase in volume, confirming the validity of the pattern.

Entry and Target Levels
- Entry Point: Traders often enter short positions (sell) upon the breakdown below the lower trendline of the rising wedge pattern.
- Stop-Loss: Place a stop-loss order above the upper trendline of the wedge pattern to manage risk.
- Target: The price target is usually set based on the height of the wedge pattern, measured from the widest point of the wedge to the breakdown point.

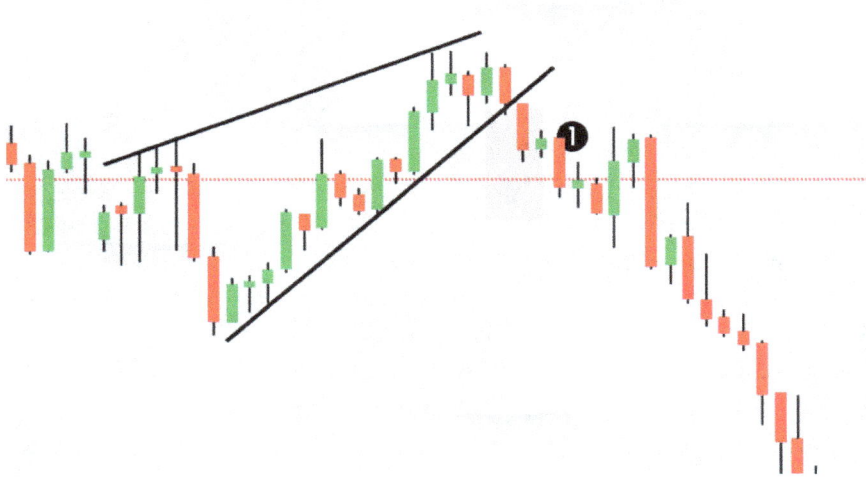

The Bullish Flag Pattern

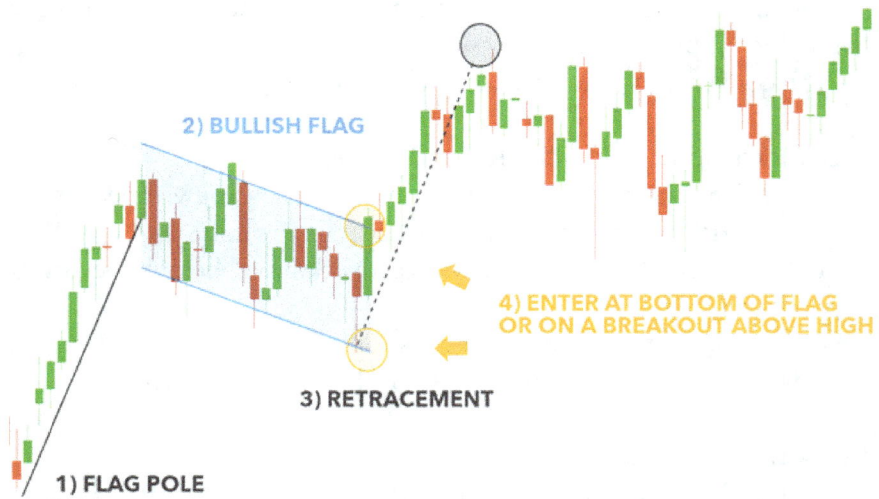

The bullish flag pattern is a continuation pattern that often occurs within the context of an uptrend. It represents a temporary pause or consolidation in price before the prevailing upward trend resumes. Here's a detailed explanation of the bullish flag pattern:

Bullish Flag Pattern Formation
1. Prior Uptrend: The bullish flag pattern typically forms after a strong upward price movement, known as the flagpole, which signifies the initial part of the uptrend.

2. Characteristics:
    - Flagpole: The flagpole is a strong, vertical price movement (upward) that precedes the flag pattern.
    - Flag: The flag portion of the pattern is a rectangular or parallelogram-shaped consolidation period, where the price moves in a sideways or slightly downward direction.

Key Elements of the Bullish Flag Pattern
-Flag Shape: The flag pattern is characterized by lower highs and lower lows within a relatively narrow price range.
-Volume: During the flag pattern, trading volume tends to decrease

compared to the volume during the flagpole.

Breakout and Trading the Bullish Flag Pattern
- Breakout Direction: The breakout from a bullish flag pattern is typically upward, indicating a continuation of the prior uptrend.
- Confirmation: Look for a decisive breakout above the upper resistance trendline of the flag pattern.
- Volume: Ideally, the breakout should be accompanied by an increase in volume, confirming the validity of the pattern.

Entry and Target Levels
- Entry Point: Traders often enter long positions (buy) upon the breakout above the upper resistance trendline of the bullish flag pattern.
- Stop-Loss: Place a stop-loss order below the lower support trendline of the flag pattern to manage risk.
- Target: The price target can be estimated based on the height of the flagpole, measured from the base of the flag to the highest point of the flagpole.

The Bearish Flag Pattern

Certainly! The bearish flag pattern is a continuation pattern that typically occurs within the context of a downtrend. It represents a temporary pause or consolidation in price before the prevailing downward trend resumes. Here's a detailed explanation of the bearish flag pattern:

Bearish Flag Pattern Formation
1. Prior Downtrend: The bearish flag pattern forms after a strong downward price movement, known as the flagpole, which signifies the initial part of the downtrend.

2. Characteristics:
   - Flagpole: The flagpole is a sharp, vertical price decline (downward) that precedes the flag pattern.
   - Flag: The flag portion of the pattern is a rectangular or parallelogram-shaped consolidation period, where the price moves in a sideways or slightly upward direction.

Key Elements of the Bearish Flag Pattern
- Flag Shape: The flag pattern is characterized by higher lows and lower highs within a relatively narrow price range.
- Volume: During the flag pattern, trading volume tends to decrease compared to the volume during the flagpole.

Breakdown and Trading the Bearish Flag Pattern
- Breakdown Direction: The breakdown from a bearish flag pattern is typically downward, indicating a continuation of the prior downtrend.
- Confirmation: Look for a decisive breakdown below the lower support trendline of the flag pattern.
- Volume: Ideally, the breakdown should be accompanied by an increase in volume, confirming the validity of the pattern.

Entry and Target Levels
- Entry Point: Traders often enter short positions (sell) upon the breakdown below the lower support trendline of the bearish flag pattern.
- Stop-Loss: Place a stop-loss order above the upper resistance trendline of the flag pattern to manage risk.
- Target: The price target can be estimated based on the height of the flagpole, measured from the base of the flag to the lowest point of the flagpole.

The bullish and Bearish rectangle

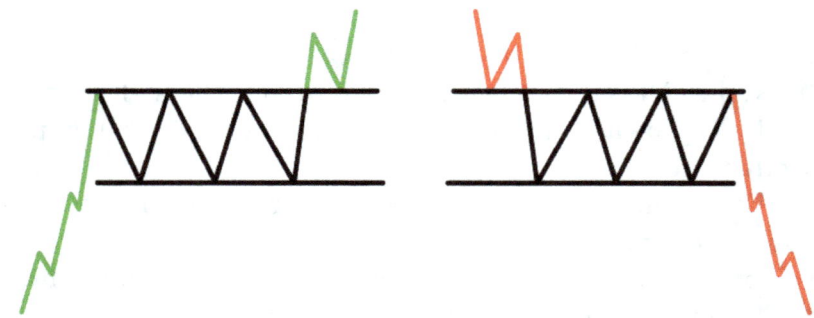

The bullish rectangle, also known as a bullish continuation rectangle, is a chart pattern that typically forms within an ongoing uptrend. It represents a consolidation or pause in price movement before the uptrend resumes. Here's a detailed explanation of the bullish rectangle pattern:

Bullish Rectangle Pattern Formation
1. Prior Uptrend: The bullish rectangle pattern forms within the context of a strong upward price movement, indicating a period of consolidation or sideways trading.

2. Characteristics:
   - Horizontal Boundary Lines: The pattern is bounded by parallel horizontal trendlines, with the upper line acting as resistance and the lower line acting as support.
   - Consolidation Phase: Price moves within the boundaries of the rectangle, forming a series of higher lows and generally maintaining a relatively stable range.

Key Elements of the Bullish Rectangle Pattern
- Shape: The rectangle pattern is characterized by a series of price highs and lows that form parallel lines, resembling a rectangle.
- Volume: During the formation of the rectangle, trading volume tends to decrease compared to the volume during the preceding uptrend.

Breakout and Trading the Bullish Rectangle Pattern
- Breakout Direction: The breakout from a bullish rectangle pattern is typically upward, signaling a continuation of the prior uptrend.
- Confirmation: Look for a decisive breakout above the upper resistance trendline of the rectangle pattern.
- Volume: Ideally, the breakout should be accompanied by an increase in volume, confirming the validity of the pattern.

Entry and Target Levels
- Entry Point: Traders often enter long positions (buy) upon the breakout above the upper resistance trendline of the bullish rectangle pattern.
- Stop-Loss: Place a stop-loss order below the lower support trendline of the rectangle pattern to manage risk.
- Target: The price target can be estimated based on the height of the rectangle pattern, measured from the support line to the resistance line.

The bearish rectangle pattern, also known as a bearish continuation rectangle, is a chart pattern that typically forms within a downtrend. It represents a period of consolidation or sideways trading before the prevailing downtrend resumes. Here's a detailed explanation of the bearish rectangle pattern:

Bearish Rectangle Pattern Formation
1. Prior Downtrend: The bearish rectangle pattern occurs within the context of a strong downward price movement, indicating a consolidation phase within the downtrend.

2. Characteristics:
   - Horizontal Boundary Lines: The pattern is bounded by parallel horizontal trendlines, with the lower line acting as support and the upper line acting as resistance.
   - Consolidation Phase: Price moves within the boundaries of the rectangle, forming a series of lower highs and generally maintaining a relatively stable range.

Key Elements of the Bearish Rectangle Pattern
- Shape: The rectangle pattern is characterized by a series of price highs and lows that form parallel lines, resembling a rectangle.
- Volume: During the formation of the rectangle, trading volume tends to decrease compared to the volume during the preceding downtrend.

Breakdown and Trading the Bearish Rectangle Pattern
- Breakdown Direction: The breakdown from a bearish rectangle pattern is typically downward, signaling a continuation of the prior downtrend.
- Confirmation: Look for a decisive breakdown below the lower support trendline of the rectangle pattern.
- Volume: Ideally, the breakdown should be accompanied by an increase in volume, confirming the validity of the pattern.

Entry and Target Levels

- Entry Point: Traders often enter short positions (sell) upon the breakdown below the lower support trendline of the bearish rectangle pattern.
- Stop-Loss: Place a stop-loss order above the upper resistance trendline of the rectangle pattern to manage risk.
- Target: The price target can be estimated based on the height of the rectangle pattern, measured from the resistance line to the support line.

The Cup And Handle Pattern

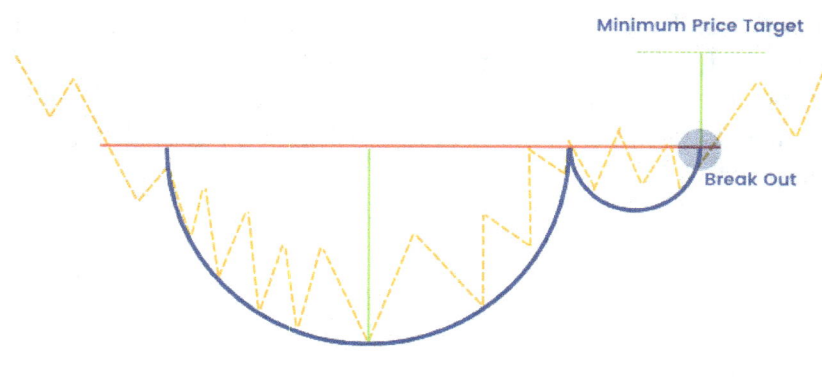

CUP & HANDEL PATTERN (REVERSAL)

The cup and handle pattern is a bullish continuation pattern that typically forms during an uptrend, signaling a potential resumption of the upward movement after a period of consolidation. Here's a detailed explanation of the cup and handle pattern:

Cup and Handle Pattern Formation
1. Cup Formation:
   - Uptrend: The cup and handle pattern begins with a strong uptrend where the price reaches a peak.
   - Cup Shape: After the peak, the price gradually declines in a rounded or U-shaped pattern resembling a cup.
   - Depth: The depth of the cup should be significant but not too deep, typically retracing 30% to 50% of the prior uptrend.

2. Handle Formation:
   - Consolidation: Following the cup formation, there is a period of consolidation where the price forms a smaller downward movement, often resembling a flag or pennant shape.
   - Handle Shape: The handle is characterized by lower highs and lower lows, forming a smaller version of the cup.

Key Elements of the Cup and Handle Pattern
- Cup Shape: A rounded bottom with a gradual decline followed by a consolidation period (the handle).
- Handle Shape: A smaller consolidation pattern within the context of the cup formation.
- Volume: During the cup formation, trading volume tends to decrease, and it should increase on the breakout from the handle.

Breakout and Trading the Cup and Handle Pattern
- Breakout Direction: The breakout from the cup and handle pattern is typically upward, indicating a continuation of the prior uptrend.
- Confirmation: Look for a decisive breakout above the resistance level formed by the handle.
- Volume: Ideally, the breakout should be accompanied by a significant increase in volume, confirming the validity of the pattern.

Entry and Target Levels
- Entry Point: Traders often enter long positions (buy) upon the breakout above the handle's resistance level.
- Stop-Loss: Place a stop-loss order below the low of the handle to manage risk.
- Target: The price target can be estimated based on the depth of the cup, measured from the lowest point of the cup to the resistance level at the handle's breakout.

The Ascending, Descending And Symmetrical Triangle Pattern

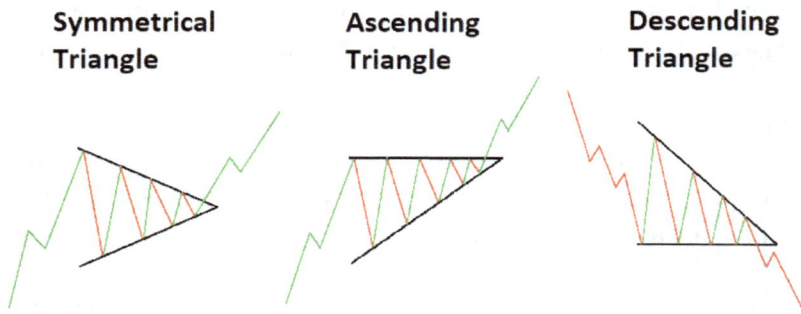

The ascending triangle, descending triangle, and symmetrical triangle are three common chart patterns in technical analysis that help traders identify potential price movements and make trading decisions. Here's an explanation of each pattern:

1. Ascending Triangle Pattern
- Definition: The ascending triangle is a bullish continuation pattern that forms during an uptrend.
- Characteristics:
  - Horizontal Resistance Line: A horizontal line acts as resistance, connecting multiple highs.
  - Rising Support Line: An ascending trendline connects higher lows, sloping upwards.
  - Triangle Shape: The pattern resembles a triangle with a flat top (resistance) and rising bottom (support).
- Breakout: The breakout from the horizontal resistance line signals a potential continuation of the uptrend.
- Volume: Ideally, volume should decrease as the pattern forms and increase on the breakout.

2. Descending Triangle Pattern
- Definition: The descending triangle is a bearish continuation pattern that forms during a downtrend.
- Characteristics:
   - Horizontal Support Line: A horizontal line acts as support, connecting multiple lows.
   - Descending Resistance Line: A descending trendline connects lower highs, sloping downwards.
   - Triangle Shape: The pattern resembles a triangle with a flat bottom (support) and declining top (resistance).
- Breakdown: The breakdown below the horizontal support line signals a potential continuation of the downtrend.
- Volume: Similar to the ascending triangle, volume should decrease as the pattern forms and increase on the breakdown.

3. Symmetrical Triangle Pattern
- Definition: The symmetrical triangle is a neutral pattern that can lead to either a bullish or bearish breakout.
- Characteristics:
   - Converging Trendlines: Both the upper and lower trendlines converge towards each other, forming a symmetrical shape.
   - Triangle Shape: The pattern has a series of lower highs (from the upper trendline) and higher lows (from the lower trendline).
- Breakout: The direction of the breakout (bullish or bearish) determines the pattern's significance.
- Volume: Volume tends to decrease as the pattern forms and typically increases on the breakout.

Trading Strategies for Triangle Patterns
- Entry: Traders often enter positions upon confirmation of a breakout (above resistance for ascending triangle, below support for descending triangle or symmetrical triangle).
- Stop-Loss: Place a stop-loss order below the breakout point (for long positions) or above the breakout point (for short positions) to manage risk.
- Target: The price target can be estimated based on the height of the triangle pattern, projected from the breakout point.

Chapter 8: Mastering Technical Indicators

A Moving Average (MA)

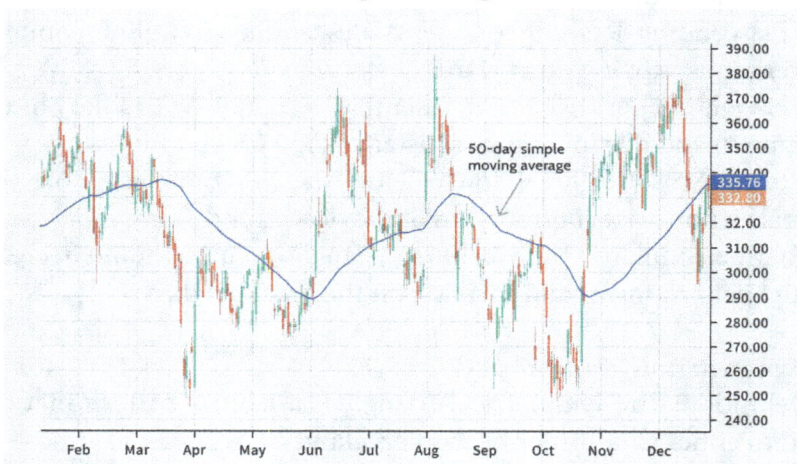

Is a widely used technical indicator in financial markets, particularly in technical analysis of stocks, forex, commodities, and other tradable assets. It is a trend-following indicator that smooths out price data by calculating the average price over a specified number of periods. The Moving Average is used to identify trends, support and resistance levels, and potential entry or exit points in trading strategies.

Types of Moving Averages:

1. Simple Moving Average (SMA):
  - The Simple Moving Average is calculated by summing up the closing prices of a security over a specified number of periods and then dividing this sum by the number of periods.
  - Formula: SMA = (Sum of Closing Prices for N Periods) / N
  - The SMA gives equal weight to each price point within the chosen period.

2. Exponential Moving Average (EMA):
   - The Exponential Moving Average gives more weight to recent price data, making it more responsive to current price movements compared to the SMA.
   - Formula: EMA = (Closing Price - EMA previous day) * (2 / (1 + N)) + EMA previous day
   - The EMA reacts more quickly to price changes, which can be beneficial for short-term trading strategies.

How Moving Averages are Used:

- Trend Identification: Moving Averages are used to identify the direction and strength of a trend. An upward-sloping MA indicates an uptrend, while a downward-sloping MA indicates a downtrend.

- Support and Resistance Levels: Moving Averages can act as dynamic support or resistance levels. In an uptrend, the MA can provide support, and in a downtrend, it can act as resistance.

- Crossovers: Moving Average crossovers, such as the crossover of a short-term MA (e.g., 20-day) above a longer-term MA (e.g., 50-day), are used to generate buy or sell signals.

- Trading Signals: Traders use Moving Averages to generate buy or sell signals based on MA crossovers, price interactions with the MA, or MA slope changes.

Example of Moving Average on a Chart:

- Simple Moving Average (SMA):
   - A 50-day SMA plotted on a price chart can help identify the long-term trend direction of a stock. If the price is above the 50-day SMA, it indicates an uptrend; if below, it indicates a downtrend.

- Exponential Moving Average (EMA):
   - A 20-day EMA and a 50-day EMA plotted together can provide short-term and long-term trend signals. A bullish crossover (20-day

EMA crossing above 50-day EMA) can signal a buy opportunity.

Moving Averages are versatile indicators that can be customized based on the trader's time horizon and trading strategy. They are essential tools for technical analysts and are often used in conjunction with other indicators to make informed trading decisions.

The Relative Strength Index (RSI)

Is a popular momentum oscillator used in technical analysis to measure the speed and change of price movements. Developed by J. Welles Wilder Jr., the RSI is one of the most widely used indicators for identifying overbought or oversold conditions in the market.

Key Components of the RSI:

- Calculation:
  - The RSI is calculated based on the average gains and losses over a specified period, typically 14 days.
  - RSI = 100 - [100 / (1 + RS)]
    - RS (Relative Strength) = Average Gain / Average Loss
    - Average Gain = (Sum of gains over N periods) / N
    - Average Loss = (Sum of losses over N periods) / N

- Range:
  - The RSI value ranges from 0 to 100.
  - Values above 70 are considered overbought, indicating that the asset may be overvalued and a reversal or correction could occur.
  - Values below 30 are considered oversold, indicating that the asset

may be undervalued and a potential buying opportunity could arise.

How RSI is Used in Trading:

- Overbought/Oversold Conditions:
  - Traders use RSI to identify extreme levels of buying (overbought) or selling (oversold) in the market. A high RSI value suggests that the price may be due for a pullback, while a low RSI value suggests a potential bounce back in price.

- Divergence:
  - RSI divergence occurs when the price of an asset forms a higher high or lower low, while the RSI forms a lower high or higher low. This can signal a potential trend reversal.

- Trend Confirmation:
  - RSI can be used to confirm the strength of a trend. In a strong uptrend, the RSI tends to stay in the overbought territory, whereas in a downtrend, the RSI tends to stay in the oversold territory.

- Signal Generation:
  - Buy Signal: When RSI crosses above 30 from below (indicating oversold conditions).
  - Sell Signal: When RSI crosses below 70 from above (indicating overbought conditions).

Example of RSI on a Chart:

- Overbought Condition:
  - If the RSI value reaches above 70, it suggests that the asset is overbought and may be due for a correction or reversal.

- Oversold Condition:
  - If the RSI value drops below 30, it suggests that the asset is oversold and may be due for a bounce back in price.

RSI is a valuable tool for traders to assess market conditions and potential trading opportunities. However, it's important to use RSI in conjunction with other technical indicators and analysis techniques to make well-informed trading decisions. Additionally, RSI settings (e.g., period length) can be adjusted based on the trader's preferences and market conditions.

The Moving Average Convergence Divergence (MACD)

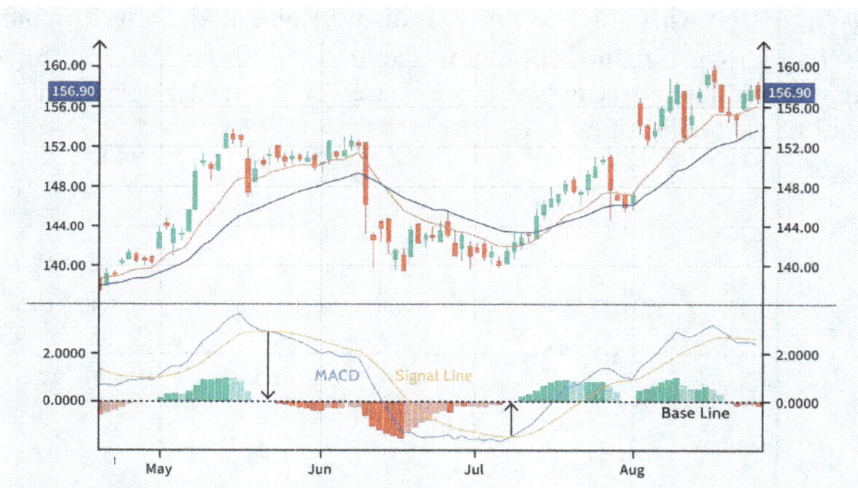

Is a popular trend-following momentum indicator used in technical analysis to identify changes in the strength, direction, momentum, and duration of a trend in an asset's price. Developed by Gerald Appel, the MACD is a versatile indicator that consists of multiple components and can be used for various trading strategies.

Components of MACD:

1. MACD Line (Moving Average Convergence Divergence Line):
   - The MACD line is calculated as the difference between the 12-period Exponential Moving Average (EMA) and the 26-period EMA.
   - Formula: MACD Line = 12-period EMA - 26-period EMA
   - The MACD line reflects the short-term momentum of the price movement.

2. Signal Line (9-period EMA of MACD Line):
   - The Signal line is a 9-period EMA of the MACD line.
   - Formula: Signal Line = 9-period EMA of MACD Line
   - The Signal line smooths out the MACD line and is used to generate buy or sell signals.

3. MACD Histogram:
  - The MACD Histogram represents the difference between the MACD line and the Signal line.
  - Formula: MACD Histogram = MACD Line - Signal Line
  - The Histogram helps visualize the difference between the MACD line and the Signal line and indicates the strength of the trend momentum.

How MACD is Used in Trading:

- MACD Line Crosses:
  - Bullish Signal: When the MACD line crosses above the Signal line (MACD line > Signal line), it indicates a potential buy signal.
  - Bearish Signal: When the MACD line crosses below the Signal line (MACD line < Signal line), it indicates a potential sell signal.

- Divergence:
  - MACD Divergence occurs when the price of the asset forms a higher high or lower low, while the MACD Histogram forms a lower high or higher low. This can signal a potential reversal in the trend.

- Zero Line Cross:
  - Bullish Signal: When the MACD line crosses above the zero line, it indicates bullish momentum.
  - Bearish Signal: When the MACD line crosses below the zero line, it indicates bearish momentum.

Example of MACD on a Chart:

-Bullish Signal:
  - If the MACD line crosses above the Signal line and the Histogram turns positive, it suggests a potential bullish trend.

- Bearish Signal:
  - If the MACD line crosses below the Signal line and the Histogram turns negative, it suggests a potential bearish trend.

MACD is a versatile indicator that can be used on different timeframes and for various trading strategies, including trend-following, momentum, and reversal strategies. Traders often use MACD in combination with other indicators and analysis techniques to confirm signals and make informed trading decisions. Adjusting the parameters (e.g., period lengths) of the MACD can customize its sensitivity to market conditions and trading preferences.

Bollinger Bands

Are a technical analysis tool developed by John Bollinger that consists of a set of three bands plotted on price charts. These bands are based on volatility and can help traders identify potential price reversals, breakouts, and overbought or oversold conditions in the market.

Components of Bollinger Bands:

1. Middle Band (Simple Moving Average - SMA):
   - The middle band is typically a 20-period Simple Moving Average (SMA) of the closing prices.
   - Formula: Middle Band = 20-period SMA

2. Upper Band (Volatility-Based Band):
   - The upper band is calculated by adding a specified number of standard deviations (usually 2) to the middle band.
   - Formula: Upper Band = Middle Band + (2 * 20-period Standard Deviation of Closing Prices)

3. Lower Band (Volatility-Based Band):
   - The lower band is calculated by subtracting a specified number of standard deviations (usually 2) from the middle band.

- Formula: Lower Band = Middle Band - (2 * 20-period Standard Deviation of Closing Prices)

Key Concepts and Usage of Bollinger Bands:

- Volatility Measurement:
  - Bollinger Bands expand and contract based on market volatility. During periods of high volatility, the bands widen, and during low volatility, the bands narrow.

- Overbought/Oversold Conditions:
  - When prices move above the upper band, it may indicate that the asset is overbought, and a reversal or pullback could occur.
  - When prices move below the lower band, it may indicate that the asset is oversold, and a rebound or bounce could occur.

- Trend Identification:
  - Bollinger Bands can help identify the direction and strength of a trend. Prices trending near the upper band suggest an uptrend, while prices near the lower band suggest a downtrend.

- Reversal and Breakout Signals:
  - Bollinger Bands can be used to identify potential reversal or breakout signals. A price breakout above the upper band or below the lower band may signal a continuation of the trend.

- Bollinger Band Squeeze:
  - A Bollinger Band squeeze occurs when the bands narrow, indicating low volatility and a potential upcoming increase in volatility and price movement.

Example of Bollinger Bands on a Chart:

- Expanding Bands:
  - During periods of high volatility, the bands widen, reflecting increased price movement and uncertainty.

- Contracting Bands:
  - During periods of low volatility, the bands narrow, indicating decreased price movement and potential consolidation.

Bollinger Bands are a versatile tool that can be used in conjunction with other technical indicators and trading strategies to analyze market conditions and make informed trading decisions. Traders often combine Bollinger Bands with momentum oscillators like the Relative Strength Index (RSI) or the Moving Average Convergence Divergence (MACD) for additional confirmation of signals. Adjusting the parameters (e.g., period length, standard deviations) of Bollinger Bands can customize their sensitivity to market conditions and trading preferences.

The Stochastic Oscillator

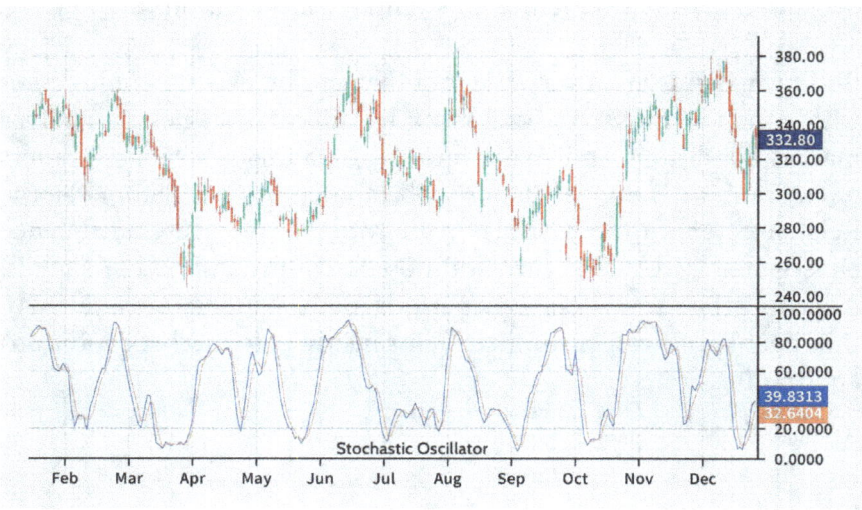

Is a popular momentum indicator used in technical analysis to identify overbought or oversold conditions in the market and to generate potential buy or sell signals. Developed by George C. Lane, the Stochastic Oscillator compares the closing price of an asset to its price range over a specified period of time.

Components of Stochastic Oscillator:

1. %K Line (Fast Stochastic)**:
   - The %K line represents the current closing price relative to the price range over a specified period (typically 14 periods).
   - Formula: %K = [(Current Close - Lowest Low) / (Highest High - Lowest Low)] * 100
      - Lowest Low: Lowest price observed over the specified period
      - Highest High: Highest price observed over the specified period

2. %D Line (Slow Stochastic)**:
   - The %D line is a moving average (typically 3-period SMA) of the %K line.

- Formula: %D = 3-period SMA of %K

Key Concepts and Usage of Stochastic Oscillator:

- Overbought/Oversold Conditions:
  - The Stochastic Oscillator ranges from 0 to 100. Readings above 80 are considered overbought, suggesting that the asset may be due for a pullback. Readings below 20 are considered oversold, suggesting that the asset may be due for a bounce back.

- Signal Generation:
  - Buy Signal: When the %K line crosses above the %D line (bullish crossover) below the oversold threshold (e.g., 20).
  - Sell Signal: When the %K line crosses below the %D line (bearish crossover) above the overbought threshold (e.g., 80).

- Divergence:
  - Stochastic Divergence occurs when the price of the asset forms a higher high or lower low, while the Stochastic Oscillator forms a lower high or higher low. This can signal a potential reversal in the trend.

- Trend Confirmation:
  - Stochastic Oscillator can be used to confirm the strength of a trend. In a strong uptrend, the Stochastic remains in overbought territory, and in a downtrend, it remains in oversold territory.

Example of Stochastic Oscillator on a Chart:

- Overbought Condition:
  - If the %K line crosses above 80, it suggests that the asset is overbought and may be due for a pullback or correction.

- Oversold Condition:
  - If the %K line drops below 20, it suggests that the asset is oversold and may be due for a bounce back or reversal in price.

Stochastic Oscillator is a versatile indicator that can be used in different timeframes and with other technical indicators to analyze market conditions and generate trading signals. Traders often use Stochastic Oscillator in combination with trend-following indicators like Moving Averages or chart patterns to confirm trading opportunities. It's important to adjust the parameters (e.g., period length) of the Stochastic Oscillator based on market conditions and trading preferences to optimize its effectiveness.

Chapter 9: Risk Management in Stock Trading

Risk management is a crucial aspect of trading in the stock market that involves strategies and techniques to minimize potential losses and preserve capital. Implementing effective risk management practices is essential for traders to navigate the inherent uncertainties and volatility of financial markets. Here are key principles and strategies for risk management while trading in the stock market:

1. Determine Risk Tolerance and Set Risk Limits:
- Assess Personal Risk Tolerance: Understand your own risk tolerance based on financial goals, investment experience, and psychological temperament.
- Define Risk Limits: Set predefined risk limits for each trade or investment based on a percentage of your total capital that you are willing to risk.

2. Use Proper Position Sizing:
- Calculate Position Size: Determine the appropriate position size for each trade based on your risk tolerance and the specific trade setup.
- Limit Exposure: Avoid risking too much capital on a single trade by adhering to position sizing rules.

3. Set Stop-Loss Orders:
- Define Exit Points: Use stop-loss orders to define exit points for trades in advance.
- Protect Capital: Stop-loss orders help limit losses by automatically exiting a position if the trade moves against you beyond a predetermined point.

4. Diversify Your Portfolio:
- Spread Risk: Diversify your investments across different asset classes, sectors, and securities to reduce concentration risk.
- Allocate Capital Wisely: Avoid putting all your capital into a single

stock or asset, which can help mitigate the impact of individual stock volatility.

5. Monitor Market Conditions:
- Stay Informed: Stay updated on market news, economic indicators, and company-specific developments that can impact stock prices.
-Adapt to Changes: Adjust risk management strategies based on evolving market conditions and new information.

6. Use Risk-Reward Ratios:
-Assess Potential Returns: Evaluate potential returns against the associated risks using risk-reward ratios.
- Seek Favorable Risk-Reward Profiles: Look for trades that offer a favorable risk-reward ratio to justify the risk taken.

7. Avoid Emotional Trading:
- Stick to Trading Plan: Follow a disciplined trading plan and avoid impulsive decisions driven by fear or greed.
- Stay Disciplined: Maintain emotional discipline by accepting losses as a natural part of trading and avoiding revenge trading.

8. Regularly Review and Adjust:
- Evaluate Performance: Regularly review trading performance and risk management practices to identify areas for improvement.
- Adapt Strategies: Adjust risk management strategies based on lessons learned from past trades and changing market conditions.

Example Scenario:
- Risk Management in Practice:
  - Assume a trader sets a risk limit of 2% of their total capital per trade.
  - If the trader's total capital is $10,000, the maximum risk per trade would be $200 (2% of $10,000).
  - Using proper position sizing and stop-loss orders, the trader ensures that no single trade risks more than $200, regardless of the outcome.

By implementing effective risk management techniques, traders can protect their capital, minimize losses during adverse market conditions, and improve the overall consistency and profitability of their trading activities. It's important to customize risk management strategies based on individual preferences, trading style, and market circumstances to optimize risk-return profiles and achieve long-term trading success.

Chapter 10: Making Money with ETFs, Mutual Funds, and IPOs

In this chapter, we will explore three popular investment vehicles—Exchange-Traded Funds (ETFs), Mutual Funds, and Initial Public Offerings (IPOs)—and discuss how investors can utilize these instruments to build wealth and achieve financial goals. Each of these investment options offers unique opportunities and considerations, making them valuable components of a diversified investment strategy.

Exchange-Traded Funds (ETFs)

Exchange-Traded Funds (ETFs) have gained significant popularity among investors due to their ease of use, diversification benefits, and cost-efficiency. ETFs are investment funds that are traded on stock exchanges, similar to individual stocks. They provide exposure to a diversified portfolio of assets, such as stocks, bonds, commodities, or a combination of asset classes. Here's how investors can make money with ETFs:

1. Diversification:
   - ETFs offer instant diversification by holding a basket of securities within a single fund. Investors can gain exposure to various market segments or asset classes without having to purchase individual stocks or bonds.

2. Low Cost:
   - ETFs generally have lower expense ratios compared to actively managed mutual funds. This cost efficiency can enhance overall investment returns over the long term.

3. Liquidity:
   - ETFs trade on major stock exchanges throughout the trading day, allowing investors to buy or sell shares at market prices. This liquidity provides flexibility and ease of trading.

4. Income Generation:
   - Some ETFs focus on income generation by investing in dividend-paying stocks or fixed-income securities. Investors can earn regular dividends or interest payments from these ETFs.

5. Capital Appreciation:
   - ETFs can appreciate in value as the underlying assets within the fund increase in price. Investors can benefit from capital appreciation through price appreciation of the ETF shares.

Mutual Funds

Mutual Funds pool money from multiple investors to invest in a diversified portfolio of securities managed by professional fund managers. Here's how investors can make money with mutual funds:

1. Professional Management:
   - Mutual funds are managed by experienced fund managers who make investment decisions based on research and analysis. This professional management can potentially lead to superior investment returns.

2. Diversification:
   - Similar to ETFs, mutual funds offer diversification across multiple securities and asset classes, reducing individual investment risk.

3. Dividend and Capital Gains:
   - Mutual funds may distribute dividends and capital gains to shareholders, providing income and potential for wealth accumulation.

4. Convenience:
   - Mutual funds offer convenience and accessibility, allowing investors to invest in various market segments and asset classes through a single fund.

5. Automatic Reinvestment:
   - Many mutual funds offer automatic dividend reinvestment and systematic investment plans (SIPs), enabling investors to compound their returns over time.

Initial Public Offerings (IPOs)

An Initial Public Offering (IPO) occurs when a private company offers its shares to the public for the first time. IPOs can present opportunities for investors to participate in the early stages of a company's growth. Here's how investors can make money with IPOs:

1. Capital Appreciation:
   - Successful IPOs can experience significant price appreciation in the secondary market if demand exceeds supply. Investors who acquire shares at the IPO price can benefit from price appreciation upon listing.

2. Early Investment in Growth Companies:
   - IPOs provide an opportunity to invest in promising companies during their early stages of growth, potentially generating substantial returns if the company succeeds.

3. Market Sentiment:
   - IPOs can reflect market sentiment and investor appetite for new offerings. Positive market sentiment and strong demand for an IPO can drive share prices higher post-listing.

4. Long-Term Investment Potential:
   - Investors with a long-term horizon may consider IPOs as part of their growth-oriented investment strategy, aiming to capitalize on the company's growth prospects over time.

Investing in ETFs, Mutual Funds, and IPOs can be integral to building a diversified investment portfolio and achieving financial objectives. Each of these investment vehicles offers distinct advantages and considerations, catering to different investment goals and risk profiles. By understanding how to leverage ETFs, Mutual Funds, and IPOs effectively, investors can optimize their investment returns and navigate the complexities of financial markets with confidence. Remember to conduct thorough research and consult with financial advisors to make informed investment decisions aligned with your financial goals and risk tolerance.

This chapter provides a comprehensive overview of how investors can make money with ETFs, Mutual Funds, and IPOs, highlighting the benefits and considerations associated with each investment option. The information presented aims to equip readers with practical insights and strategies for incorporating these investment vehicles into their overall investment approach.

Chapter 11: 5 Free tools For intraday trading

Intraday trading requires real-time data, analysis, and quick decision-making. There are several free online tools available that can assist intraday traders in making informed decisions. Here is a list of five free online tools for intraday trading, along with descriptions of their key features:

1. TradingView
 - Key Features:
   - Advanced charting platform with customizable technical indicators and drawing tools.
   - Real-time market data for stocks, forex, cryptocurrencies, and more.
   - Social networking features for sharing trading ideas and strategies.
   - Accessible via web browser or mobile app (iOS and Android).

2. Investing.com
 - Key Features:
   - Live quotes, charts, and technical analysis tools for stocks, indices, commodities, and currencies.
   - Economic calendar with real-time updates on important economic events and indicators.
   - News and analysis from financial experts.
   - Customizable watchlists to track favorite assets.

3. Yahoo Finance
 - Key Features:
   - Detailed stock quotes, historical data, and interactive charts.
   - News and analysis from leading financial publications.
   - Portfolio tracking and customizable watchlists.
   - Accessible via web browser and mobile app (iOS and Android).

4. StockCharts.com
 - Key Features:
   - Wide range of technical analysis tools and charting options.
   - Predefined technical scans to identify potential trading opportunities.
   - Educational resources and tutorials on technical analysis.
   - Free access to basic features, with premium options available for additional functionality.

5. Finviz
 - Key Features:
   - Stock screener with customizable filters based on technical and fundamental criteria.
   - Interactive charts with advanced technical analysis tools.
   - Heatmaps and visual representations of market data.
   - News aggregator for tracking market-moving headlines.

These free online tools provide intraday traders with valuable resources for analyzing market trends, identifying trading opportunities, and staying informed about key developments. It's important for traders to explore these tools and determine which ones best suit their trading style and objectives. Additionally, while these tools are free to use, traders should always exercise caution and conduct thorough research before making trading decisions based on the information provided.

NOTES

NOTES

NOTES

NOTES